The Waiting

An Overview of the New Testament: Part Two

Bob Evely

To Jill

The wife of my youth.
My best friend.
Most definitely my better half.
An amazing wife, mother, and grandma.

You have made this spiritual journey with me,
Every step of the way.

You have always supported me in all that I do.

I appreciate you far more
than words could possibly express.

With love,

Bob

"The Waiting"
Abby Evely

"The Waiting"
Elinor Evely

An Overview of the New Testament: Part Two

The Waiting

"The Fellowship of Jewish Believers"

Acts (Part 1)
Hebrews
James
Peter (1st and 2nd)
John (1st, 2nd and 3rd)
Jude

"Be watching, then, for you are not aware on what day
your Lord is coming." (Matthew 24:42)

Bob Evely.

*Scriptures taken from the Concordant Literal New Testament
and the Concordant Version of the Old Testament unless otherwise noted.
Concordant Publishing Concern, 15570 West Knochaven Road,
Santa Clarita, CA 91387 (www.Concordant.org)*

Grace Evangel Fellowship:
P O Box 6, Wilmore, KY 40390
www.GraceEvangel.org

The Waiting; An Overview of the New Testament – Part Two
by Bob Evely
Copyright © 2018 by Robert W. Evely

First Printing: 2018

ISBN 978-1-7323228-7-5

Cover created by Cris Evely
Front: Lilli Evely, Abby Evely
Back: The Evely girls

Published by:
Robert W. Evely
P.O. Box 6
Wilmore, KY 40390

www.GraceEvangel.org

Table of Contents

Opening Remarks

If the Bible is God's Word ... truth revealed by God to mankind ... then we cannot shy away from proclaiming it. But it is important that we are proclaiming the correct message.

Isn't it concerning that there are hundreds of different Christian denominations, and thousands upon thousands of individual churches; and they are often declaring truth from God's Word that is conflicting. As those of the world observe this great confusion they come to one of several conclusions:

1. The Bible is not the revealed Word of God, as its content is often conflicting and the truths espoused by Christians does not make sense.

2. The Bible might be the Word of God, but it is impossible to really understand it, as there are so many different learned people that disagree and argue about what it says.

3. The Bible might be the Word of God, but there are many different translations and versions to buy and they often disagree with one another.

There are variations as well, but these three major categories encompass much of what those of the world are thinking.

So it is important to really understand exactly what the Bible says, and what it means, so as to avoid creating even more confusion when we share truth with the world. There are MANY who know what the Bible says; at least the version of the Bible they have chosen. Many even memorize large portions of the Bible. BUT ... even more important than knowing what the Bible says is knowing what it means! Interpretation and application! It is the wide array of interpretation and application that creates confusion.

What follows is an overview of the Greek Scriptures; often called the New Testament. This is not intended to be a verse by verse commentary. It is an overview; an examination of the writer's train of thought, with a consideration toward how all parts of the Bible fit together and the meaning being relayed to mankind in this present age. Verse by verse commentaries have a purpose, but care must be taken not to lose sight of the forest as we study the trees. This is intended to be an examination of the forest.

Each section begins with an overview; a broad flow of the text. Often this is my own paraphrase; though words that are *italicized* are direct quotations from the Concordant Version (unless otherwise noted). Interspersed in a different font and indented are my own notes and observations. These comments represent my personal observations based on my own study of the Scriptures and, at times, a consideration of many different commentators. But I would caution the reader ... do not believe my interpretations just because you think they make sense. Read and study the Scriptures for yourself! Beware of any preacher, teacher, or scholar who tells you they have it all figured out. Again; there are MANY preachers, teachers, and scholars who read the same Bible but who come to different conclusions.

Near the end of their lives, the apostles (particularly Peter and Paul) noted that false teachers had infiltrated the church and were leading people away from the truth. Paul, in his final writings, stressed the importance of passing the truth to *faithful men*. The church was in a state of apostasy, or falling away. Most had abandoned the apostles even in their lifetimes. So as the church entered those first few centuries following the death of the apostles it is more likely that doctrine incorporated much tradition and falsehood ... for this had begun even while the apostles lived.

All this to say ... trust no preacher, teacher, or scholar ... no matter how learned and trustworthy they appear. Seek truth from the Scriptures themselves, using helps available to be sure you penetrate through even the biases of the translators. Study, and think for yourself.

With this being said, let us proceed to consider the Greek Scriptures; seeking to understand the truth God has revealed to us for this present day!

𝔄𝔠𝔱𝔰 (𝔓𝔞𝔯𝔱 𝔒𝔫𝔢)

An Overview of the Scriptures, by
BOB EVELY © 2018.
An Independent Minister of Christ Jesus,
Of the church at Wilmore, Kentucky

The four "Gospels" (Matthew, Mark, Luke, John) give an account of the time when Jesus walked upon the earth. In those accounts we see Jesus (the king) proclaiming that the kingdom is near; referring to the restoration of the kingdom unto Israel. His audience was Israel!

But Israel would not receive her king. Jesus is crucified; and the kingdom is rejected. As Acts begins will the good news go now to the Gentiles instead of the Jews?

A close study of Acts is key in understanding the difference between the *expectation* and the *message* proclaimed to Israel, and the *expectation* and the *message* later proclaimed to the Body of Christ. By *expectation* I mean; what was the audience expecting or looking for in their future as they heard the message proclaimed?

Keeping this in mind let us begin our study of Acts.

CHAPTER 1

Post resurrection appearances (1:1)

After the resurrection, Jesus appears upon the earth for a period of forty days; teaching His disciples things concerning *the kingdom of God*. Jesus directs the apostles to remain in Jerusalem, waiting *for the promise of the Father*. He tells them that as John baptized in water, they will be *baptized in holy spirit*.

> This is immediately after the gospel accounts. Remember Jesus' message concerning the kingdom of God; He was preparing Israel for the kingdom's restoration upon the earth. Thus far we have seen nothing that would alter that message.

Restoring the kingdom? (1:6)

The apostles ask, Art thou at this time restoring the kingdom to Israel? Jesus replies, *Not yours is it to know times or eras which the Father placed in His own jurisdiction*.

Copyright 2018, Robert W. Evely, Wilmore, KY

When will the kingdom be restored unto ISRAEL?

Observe that Jesus does not tell them the kingdom will NOT be restored TO ISRAEL, but that it is not theirs to know the timing. We can infer, then, that the kingdom will indeed be restored *to Israel,* and we will see this occur when Christ returns in Revelation. But the TIME for this to happen is not yet revealed.

Jesus tells them when the holy spirit comes on them and empowers them, they shall be His WITNESSES *both in Jerusalem and in entire Judea and Samaria, and as far as the limits of the earth.*

This, then, will be the mission of the apostles; to be HIS WITNESSES.

Ascension (1:9)

As Jesus ascends from the mount called Olivet, two men tell those gathered, *This Jesus Who is being taken up from you into heaven shall come thus, in the manner in which you gaze at Him going into heaven.*

As He *physically* ascended, He will *physically* return to the earth. This is the expectation of the believers among Israel; Christ's return to the earth to reign.

Waiting in Jerusalem (1:12)

Obediently they wait in Jerusalem, persevering with one accord in prayer. There are about 120 of them. As they wait, Judas is replaced by Matthias who is *numbered with the eleven apostles.*

What is the requirement for Judas' replacement? One who was *with us in all the time in which the Lord Jesus came in and out to us, beginning from the baptism of John until the day on which He was taken up from us.* The mission for the apostles is *to become a witness of His resurrection.* (1:22)

OBSERVE THE IMPORTANCE OF KEEPING THE NUMBER OF APOSTLES AT TWELVE!

Remember that the mission of the Twelve is to go to the tribes of Israel, just as Jesus had done throughout His lifetime. Jesus was not commissioned to go to all nations, but only to Israel. That was His commission. It is interesting to note that there were twelve tribes in Israel, and twelve apostles commissioned to go to Israel. It is also interesting that later, when Paul becomes an apostle, he is IN ADDITION TO THE TWELVE. He is never one of the Twelve! This makes sense as Paul's mission was different ... to go to the Gentiles. Paul will become an apostle of a different kind, with a different assignment. Keep this in mind as we continue our study through the New Testament.

CHAPTER 2

Pentecost [(2:1)]

At Pentecost, Israelites from all nations assemble in Jerusalem. They are *filled with holy spirit, and begin to speak in different languages, according as the spirit gave them to declaim.*

> # Pentecost was a gathering of ISRAEL

This was not the first Pentecost. This was the annual feast of Pentecost that was drawing ISRAELITES from all regions to Jerusalem. What an appropriate occasion, with all assembled, for what God had in store.

The Jews had come from *every nation under heaven.* They are confused, for they each heard them speaking in their own vernacular. Peter tells them this is what the prophet Joel had declared (Joel 2:28-32); *I shall be pouring out from My spirit on all flesh ... Your sons and daughters shall prophesy.* Peter also tells his audience things that will come to pass at some future time.

✓ *Miracles in heaven above, and signs on the earth below*
✓ *Blood and fire and vapor pillars of smoke*
✓ *The sun turned into darkness and the moon into blood*
✓ *Ere the coming of the day of the Lord, the great and advent day*
✓ *And it shall be that everyone, whosoever should be invoking the name of the Lord shall be saved.*

So while a part of Joel's prophecy was being fulfilled on that Pentecost, other parts of the prophecy were to be fulfilled at some future time, *ere the coming of the day of the Lord.*

Peter addresses the assembled Israelites [(2:22)]

Peter begins by reminding them, You assassinated Jesus, a Man demonstrated to be from God by powerful deeds and miracles and signs. God raised Him; it was not possible for Him to be held by death. *We are all witnesses ... this Jesus, God raises. Exalted to the right hand of God, He obtained the promise of the holy spirit from the Father, and He pours out this which you are observing and hearing.*

Let all the HOUSE OF ISRAEL *know that God makes Him Lord as well as Christ, this Jesus Whom you crucify.*

Let "the house of ISRAEL" know

Although Jesus, the Christ and King, has been rejected by the Jews and crucified, even at this point the evangel being proclaimed by the apostles is still going only to THE HOUSE OF ISRAEL. (2:36)

When asked what they should we be doing, Peter responds, *Repent and be baptized each of you in the name of Jesus Christ, for the pardon of your sins, and you shall be obtaining the gratuity of the holy spirit. To you is the promise, and to your children, and to all those afar, whosoever the Lord our God should be calling to Him. Be saved from this crooked generation.*

To recap thus far; the *gospel* (good news) is being proclaimed TO ISRAEL. The restoration of the kingdom unto Israel, upon the earth, is still anticipated and still lies ahead. The call is to REPENT *to those God shall be calling.* And to this point He is calling only the house of Israel.

To be *saved* means to be saved to experience life within the kingdom once it is restored upon the earth.

Life in the ecclesia [(2:41)]

After the events of Pentecost there were about 3000 souls added to the ecclesia, and *the Lord was adding to those being saved daily.* The ecclesia is persevering:

✓ In the teaching of the apostles,

- ✓ In fellowship,
- ✓ In the breaking of bread,
- ✓ In prayers.

Many MIRACLES and SIGNS occur thru the apostles in Jerusalem. They are all in the same place, and

- ✓ Have all things in common
- ✓ Divide possessions as some would have need
- ✓ Persevere day by day in the sanctuary (place outside the temple proper, open to the Jewish public)
- ✓ Break bread in homes
- ✓ Eat with exultation and simplicity of heart

LET'S STOP AND THINK ABOUT A FEW THINGS ...

ECCLESIA: The *ecclesia* (commonly translated "church" in most versions) consisted only of Israelites at this point. They met in the sanctuary. Consider Acts 21:28 where the Jews become enraged when they think Paul had taken a Gentile into the sanctuary. Take care when attempting to apply things we are reading thus far in Acts to our present age. The *gospel* at this time is going out only to Israel, and the *ecclesia* (church) consists only of Israelites.

Ecclesia is the word found in the original New Testament Greek. It simply means *out-called ones*, or those who have been *called out* from the whole of mankind for some particular purpose. Ecclesia does not always mean the same thing in every context, and most modern Bible translations confuse things by using the word church; causing us to think that all instances are talking directly to or about the church as we know it today. As we read on we must remember that at this point in Acts the *ecclesia* is comprised only of Israelites. They are the ones *called out* by God at this point.

DISTINCTIONS IN GOD'S WORD: Observing the distinctions in the Scriptures between that which is spoken to Israel and that which is spoken to the Body of Christ is, I believe, to *correctly cut* (or in some translations *rightly divide*) the Word of God. (2 Timothy 2:15) Some will say that to divide the Scriptures into *dispensations* or *eras* is to destroy the unity of God's Word. I contend that failing to take note of differences between various dispensations or eras and forcing all of Scripture to apply directly to us today, is to cloud and distort the revelation that God has entrusted to us.

PENTECOST: Many teach that the church was born at Pentecost. (Acts 2) But we must remember that Pentecost was a Jewish feast, and the ecclesia ("church") we read about in Acts 2 consists exclusively of Jews.

SALVATION: When we read about those being *saved* we must consider what they were being saved *from* at this point. If you have spent much time within an organized church you have probably come to think you know what "saved" means. But in the Scriptures to be saved may mean different things, so we must examine the context and consider the circumstances of those being mentioned at any given point. "Saved" might mean being saved from death (rescued from the enemy in battle), or healed (saved from death), or saved from the anticipated indignation of God or tribulation which is to come. Being saved *never* means salvation from eternal torment, since the doctrine of eternal torment is a fabrication of man's teachings and is not found within the Word of God. The common thread we see in being "saved" is salvation from death (in battle, in disease or from God's wrath at some future time either just prior to Christ's return, or upon His return).

THE KINGDOM: Remember that the prophets had foretold the coming day of the Lord, when the Messiah would return to judge the world. This is the kingdom that is to come upon the earth. It was rejected by the Jews when Christ was crucified, but it is still anticipated at some future point. Before the ascension the apostles asked Jesus if the time had come for the kingdom to be restored to Israel. This was their expectation, but the time had not yet come. *Not yours is it to know times or eras which the Father placed in His own jurisdiction.* (1:6) Still, it is this "kingdom evangel" that is being proclaimed, just as Jesus had proclaimed it. *Repent ... the kingdom is near.* And when the king returns, and when the kingdom is restored unto Israel, there will come the time of judging. And so at this point Peter is proclaiming that now is the time to repent and prepare for the king Who will come and judge. *Repent and be saved from His wrath and judgment.*

CHAPTER 3

Healing [(3:1)]

Peter heals a lame man. Those who see him walking and praising God are filled with awe and amazement.

In Jesus' earthly ministry signs and wonders closely accompanied the proclaiming of the kingdom evangel. We see this continuing in the time of the apostles; the *Pentecostal administration.* This is how God was operating as the kingdom evangel was being proclaimed to Israel. But can we legitimately assume that God *must* be operating in the same way today? Israel was promised earthly blessings; land, physical blessings and curses based on obedience, and the restoration of the kingdom upon the earth. Does it not make sense that the proclamation of these things TO ISRAEL would be accompanied by physical signs and wonders upon this earth?

But is the expectation for the Body of Christ in this present age the same? No; we have been promised spiritual blessings, and our expectation is not for the kingdom to be restored upon this earth, but for a celestial kingdom; and for Christ to call us upward to meet Him in the air where we will serve Him in the celestial realm. (1 Thessalonians 4:13ff) With *spiritual* promises and expectations can we rightly assume we will be given *earthly* signs and wonders? Is not His grace sufficient, as Paul learned, without signs and wonders?

Consider this. Timothy suffered *often infirmities.* (1 Timothy 5:23) There was no prayer for healing; he was prescribed wine. Epaphroditus was sick and close to death, yet Paul did not attempt to heal him. He even left Trophimus at Miletum sick. Why did Paul not pray for his healing?

These are just some things to think about for our studies of Paul's epistles. For now I simply ask you to consider; can we rightly assume that God is operating the same in our present age as He was operating in the days of Acts?

Peter addresses those gathered ^(3:11)

As the entire people run to Peter and John at Solomon's portico, Peter addresses those gathered. He asks, Why do you look at us as if we did this by our own power or devoutness?

> Here is a hint as to why these miraculous events took place at the Pentecost gathering; to grab attention and to demonstrate God's power.

The God of our fathers glorifies Jesus, Whom you kill, and Whom God rouses from among the dead ... of which we are witnesses.

> Remember, Peter is addressing the Israelites. And in his sharing the heart of the gospel message for his day we see the mission of Peter and the other apostles; they are *witnesses.* Peter's message; that Jesus was roused from among the dead by God; was to cause Israel to BELIEVE that Jesus was, in fact, the Son of God and the Christ (Messiah). And by adding, *What God announces before through the prophets, the suffering of His Christ, He thus*

fulfills; Peter is citing the Old Testament Scriptures in support of his argument to Israel.

Peter then shares some additional things with his audience (Israel):

✓ Repent, *then, and turn about for the erasure of your sins,*

✓ *So that* seasons of refreshing *should be coming from the face of the Lord,*

✓ *And He should* dispatch the one *fixed upon before for you, Christ Jesus,*

✓ *Whom heaven must indeed receive* until the times of restoration of all.

The message to Israel has not changed

Observe that following the death and resurrection of Jesus, the message to Israel has not changed. Israel awaits the restoration of the kingdom upon the earth, as in the days of King David. We recall that Jesus proclaimed, *Repent; the kingdom is near.* Peter now proclaims, *Repent; that Christ will return from heaven and seasons of refreshing will be coming.* (In other words, that the kingdom would come upon the earth, as it is in heaven.)

It is important to pause and consider the message being proclaimed at this juncture. IF ISRAEL WILL REPENT, CHRIST WILL RETURN AND THE KINGDOM WILL BE RESTORED TO ISRAEL.

Moses had said God would raise up a prophet from within Israel, and all the prophets announced *these days. You are the sons of the prophets and of the covenant which God covenanted with your fathers saying to Abraham: And in your seed all the kindreds of the earth shall be blessed.*

So the appearance of the Messiah (Christ) had been foretold by Moses and the prophets. We also see in these words a reminder of God's promise to ultimately bless all people. (Genesis 12:3)

To you first, God, raising His Boy, commissions Him to bless you by turning away each of you from your wickedness. (3:26)

Here is yet another reminder that at this point (Acts 3) God's Word is going specifically TO ISRAEL, with the intent that they turn from their wickedness (repent) and recognize (believe) that Jesus, whom they crucified, is indeed the Christ.

CHAPTER 4

Peter and John are arrested (4:1)

The leaders of Israel (priests, officer of the sanctuary, Sadducees) are exasperated because of their teaching and announcing the resurrection of Jesus. They take Peter and John into custody.

Many hear the word and believe (4:4)

The number of men grows to about 5000.

> THE NUMBER IS GROWING. As was the case when Jesus' ministry was at its peak, many are hearing, observing the signs and wonders, and believing. Remember, if the people will repent, Christ will return and the kingdom upon the earth will come.
>
> But despite the growing numbers, the Jewish leaders continue to oppose the evangel, as was the case in Jesus' day.

Peter's speech when questioned (4:5)

If you are asking how the infirm man was *saved*, let it be known to you and to the entire PEOPLE OF ISRAEL that in the name of Jesus Christ, the Nazarene, Whom you crucify, Whom God rouses from among the dead, in this name the man stands before you sound.

> # Peter's remarks are directed to the people of Israel!

> SAVED? Here the word *saved* is used to indicate *healed*, for the man was *saved* from his infirmity. When we see the word *saved* we must be sure to ask its meaning from the context. Who is being saved? What is he being saved from? What is meant by salvation in the context?

This is the Stone that is being scorned by you builders, which is becoming the head of the corner. There is no salvation in any other one, for neither is there any other name given under heaven among men, in which we must be saved.

> Many will claim that this verse offers proof of the necessity of believing in Christ Jesus in this lifetime to be saved. Certainly Christ is needed for

> salvation. Without Him NONE would be saved. But because of Him, NONE will ultimately be lost.

They order Peter and John to stop teaching in the name of Jesus. They reply, We cannot but be speaking of what we perceive and hear. Peter and John are released as the leaders can find no grounds to be chastening them, because of the people. For they all glorified God for this *sign of healing* that had occurred.

Prayer for boldness (4:23)

Herod and Pilate, together with the nations and the peoples of Israel, gather against Jesus *to do whatever Thy hand and Thy counsel designates beforehand to occur.*

> While it was the Jews and the nations that gathered to crucify Jesus, we note here that these events were designated by God to occur. Here we see the workings of God's will, and man's will.

> It is not that man's will is taken away, or even limited. Man makes use of his will to accomplish the ultimate evil; the assassination of the Son of God. But the execution of man's will cannot prevent God's will from being accomplished. At the crucifixion man thought he was in full control. Yet thru these events, and unbeknownst to man, God is accomplishing His will.

Endow Thy slaves with all boldness to be speaking Thy word, stretching out Thy hand for healing and signs and miracles, thru the name of Jesus. The place where they gathered is shaken. They are all filled with the holy spirit and speak the word of God with boldness.

Life in the ecclesia (4:32)

All possessions are held in common. With great power the apostles give testimony to the resurrection of Jesus Christ, the Lord. Great grace is on them all. There are no indigent among them, for they sell their possessions and the apostles distribute to each as they have need.

CHAPTER 5

Ananias and Sapphira (5:1)

Ananias sells an acquisition and embezzles from the price, bringing only a *part* of it to the apostles. He *falsified* to the holy spirit. Peter tells him, You do not lie to men, but to God. Ananias hears these words and *falls down, giving up the soul.*

Sapphira later comes and also lies when questioned by Peter. Peter asks, Why is it that you agreed to try the spirit of the Lord? She also falls *and gives up the soul.*

Great fear came on the whole ecclesia and on all who hear these things.

> Would the same happen today? During the "Pentecostal Administration" we see God immediately meting out judgment to Ananias and Sapphira for lying to Him. In this current "Administration of Grace" does God work the same way?

Many signs, wonders and healings (5:12)

Through the hands of the apostles many signs and miracles occur among the people. Multitudes are added to those believing, and they carry the infirm into the squares seeking to have Peter's shadow come upon them. They come also from the cities about Jerusalem, with the infirm and those molested by unclean spirits, all of whom are cured.

> While many saw the signs and miracles and *believed,* we read that *no one dared to join them.* (5:13) This seems to be a parallel to the days of Jesus' ministry when the multitudes believed His words and flocked to see the signs and wonders, but not many were willing to pay the cost to follow.

Apostles are jailed, and released by a messenger (5:17)

During the night a messenger opens the doors of the jail, saying, *Go, and, standing in the sanctuary, speak to the people all the declarations of this life.*

When the Sanhedrin and entire senate of the sons of Israel are gathered, they find the prisoners are no longer there. They find the apostles in the sanctuary, teaching, and they lead them before the Sanhedrin.

Before the Sanhedrin (5:27)

When challenged about continuing to teach in Jesus' name, Peter and the apostles reply that one must yield to God rather than to men.

The God of our fathers rouses Jesus. This *Inaugerator and Saviour* God exalts to His right hand, *to give repentance* TO ISRAEL and the *pardon of sins.* We are witnesses to these declarations, as well as the holy spirit which God gives to those yielding to Him.

To give repentance to ISRAEL

> Still at this point we see that the purpose of the evangel being proclaimed by the apostles is to reach ISRAEL; specifically *to give repentance to Israel and the pardon of sins.*

Gamaliel's wisdom [(5:33)]

The Jewish leaders intend to assassinate them, but Gamaliel (a Pharisee in the Sanhedrin and a teacher of the law) advises; *Withdraw from these men and let them be. If this work is of men, it will be demolished. But if it is of God, you will not be able to demolish them, lest you may be found fighting against God.*

They charge the apostles not to speak in the name of Jesus, and release them. The apostles rejoice that they were deemed worthy to be dishonored for the sake of the Name.

Teaching daily [(5:42)]

Every day, in the sanctuary and home by home, they teach and bring the evangel of Jesus Christ

CHAPTER 6

Dissension arises in the ecclesia [(6:1)]

The Hellenists complain against the Hebrews, that their widows are being overlooked at the daily dispensation. The Twelve call the multitude of the disciples and instruct the brethren to choose seven attested men, full of the spirit and wisdom, to serve, allowing the Twelve to focus on the word of God. Stephen is chosen as one of the seven.

> The Hellenists were Jews who had accepted Greek customs.

Many disciples, including some Priests [(6:7)]

The word of God grows. The number of disciples in Jerusalem multiplies tremendously. And a vast throng of the priests *obeyed the faith.*

Stephen is apprehended [(6:8)]

Stephen does great miracles and signs among the people. None can withstand the wisdom and the spirit with which he speaks. They claim he blasphemed Moses and God, stirring up the people, elders and scribes.

Stephen is led before the Sanhedrin. False witnesses are put on the stand, saying that he is making declarations against the holy place and the law, and saying that Jesus will be changing the customs of Moses.

CHAPTER 7

Stephen's speech (7:1)

After recounting a history of Israel, Stephen directs accusations against those gathered. They are stiff-necked and uncircumcised in their hearts and ears; ever clashing with the holy spirit. As their fathers did, they persecute the prophets and kill those who came to announce the coming of the *Just One,* of Whom they have become traitors and murderers.

They stone Stephen. SAUL WAS ENDORSING HIS ASSASSINATION.

> Note the use of the word ECCLESIA in Stephen's speech. (7:38) He is referring to a "gathering" in the wilderness in Moses' day. *Ecclesia* is translated *church* in most every case, but here is one example where ecclesia certainly does not mean church. Even the modern translators use another word here. (Also see Acts 19:32,40,41.)
>
> *Ecclesia* simply means a group of people *called-out* from a larger group. (ek = out; klesia = called). *Ecclesia* does not always mean the same thing, as is clearly displayed in the current example. We cannot, therefore, assume the *ecclesia* (called-out-ones) that Jesus spoke of in the Gospels, or the *ecclesia* referred to early in Acts (which was primarily Jewish), is the same as the *ecclesia* Paul later speaks of.
>
> When we read of the *ecclesia* in God's Word (you'll find the word *church* in most translations, which is misleading), we should always ask which *ecclesia* (out-called group of people) is being referred to. We cannot simply take all cases where *ecclesia* is used and use this as the model for our present-day *church.*

CHAPTER 8

Great persecution (8:1)

In that day there came to be a great persecution of the ecclesia in Jerusalem, and they were dispersed among the districts of Judea and Samaria, except the apostles. SAUL DEVASTATED THE ECCLESIA, going into homes to drag out men and women; giving them over to jail. Those who are dispersed evangelize with the word.

Philip evangelizes in Samaria (8:5)

Philip is bringing *the evangel concerning the kingdom of God and the name of Jesus Christ.* (8:12) The throngs heed the things being said by Philip, on hearing them and observing THE SIGNS which he did. Many spirits are cast out, and many are cured.

Simon had amazed Samaria with his magic. Now he believes and is baptized.

Peter and John are sent to Samaria (8:14)

Hearing that Samaria had received the word of God, the apostles in Jerusalem send Peter and John who come and pray so they might obtain the holy spirit. They had been baptized, but the holy spirit had not yet *fallen on any of them*. Peter and John place their hands on them, and they obtain holy spirit.

Simon asks to buy authority (8:18)

Simon offers the apostles money that he might have the authority to lay-on hands to give the holy spirit. Peter tells him, May your silver be for destruction together with you, seeing that you infer that the gratuity of God is to be acquired by means of money. Repent from this evil of yours, and beseech the Lord, if consequently the notion of your heart will be forgiven you.

Villages of the Samaritans are evangelized (8:25)

Philip and the Ethiopian Eunuch (8:26)

Philip *evangelizes to him Jesus* and baptizes him. The Lord snatches away Philip, and he is found in Azotus where he brings the evangel to all the cities until he comes to Caesarea.

CHAPTER 9

Saul's conversion (9:1)

On the road to Damascus, Saul is blinded for three days, and does not eat or drink. A voice from heaven says, *He is a choice instrument of Mine, to bear my name before both the nations and kings, besides the sons of Israel...*

> This occurs in 36 A.D. Note the two parts to Paul's commission. He is to bear Christ's name before:
>
> ✓Nations and kings (i.e. the nations), and
>
> ✓The sons of Israel
>
> Unlike the Twelve who are commissioned to go only to Israel, Paul has a dual commission. He is the ONLY apostle commissioned to go to the nations; but note that he is ALSO commissioned to go to the sons of Israel. We must keep this in mind as we continue our review of Acts, and when we read Paul's epistles. We must always ask; is this word being spoken to the nations or to

Israel? Paul was commissioned to go to both; and we cannot assume the message he bears will be the same in both cases. In fact we will see huge differences in the message Paul (and the others) proclaims to Israel, and the message Paul proclaims to the nations.

Saul's ministry begins (9:19)

Saul comes to be with the disciples in Damascus for some days. Immediately in the synagogues he heralds Jesus, that He is the Son of God. The Jews of Damascus are confused as Saul *deduces* that Jesus is the Christ, and they consult to assassinate him. The disciples lower Saul thru the wall in a hamper. (See 2 Corinthians 11:32)

Coming to Jerusalem Saul spends time with the disciples. (Galatians 1:18-19) He speaks boldly with the Hellenists, and they try to assassinate him. The brethren lead him into Caesarea, and they send him to Tarsus.

Not immediately to Jerusalem? From Galatians 1:17 we learn that in these early days Saul went to Arabia and then back to Damascus; before going to Jerusalem. He makes it clear that the evangel he proclaims was not received from men but came thru a revelation of Jesus Christ. (Galatians 1:12)

Had Saul's (Paul's) message been the same as that being declared by the other apostles, he would logically have gone first to spend time with the others. But he makes it very clear that this was not the case.

Paul's "my evangel" was not just the same message going to a different group of people (the Gentiles). He was entrusted with the evangel *of* the Uncircumcision, while Peter was entrusted with the evangel *of* the Circumcision. (Galatians 2:7)

Saul spoke with the Jews in Damascus, *deducing* that Jesus is the Christ. (9:22) *Deducing* is *sumbibazo* in the Greek; the same word translated *unite* when speaking of the physical realm. To *deduce* is to unite the various facts into a single conclusion. Paul was presenting to the Jews the various evidences in support of the conclusion that Jesus is the Christ. This give us a glimpse into a method used by Saul/Paul as he evangelizes.

The ecclesia enjoys peace (9:31)

The ecclesia in all of Judea, Galilee and Samaria has peace, being edified, and goes on in the fear of the Lord and the consolation of the holy spirit. The numbers multiply.

Miracles ^(9:32)

Peter heals Eneas, the Paralytic. All those dwelling at Lydda and Saron are aware of him and turn back to the Lord.

Peter raises Tabitha from the dead. Tabitha is a disciple full of good acts and alms. This miracle becomes known in all of Joppa, and many *believe on the Lord*.

CHAPTER 10

Cornelius – Peter's visions ^(10:1)

Cornelius is a centurion of a squadron called "Italian," devout and fearing God with his entire house. He does many alms to the people and beseeches God continually. He is told, Your prayers and alms have ascended for a memorial in front of God.

An *ecstasy* comes on Peter. He beholds heaven opened and is told, What God cleanses do not count contaminating. Three men are seeking you. Go with them and doubt nothing, for I have commissioned them.

Peter goes with the men and tells Cornelius, You know it is illicit for a Jew to join or to come to another tribe. God shows me not to say that any man is contaminating or unclean. I grasp that God is not partial, but *in every nation he who is fearing Him and acting righteously is acceptable to Him.*

You are aware that God dispatches to the sons of Israel, bringing the evangel of peace through Jesus Christ Who is Lord of all. We are witnesses of all that He does. He charges us to herald to the people and certify that this is He Who is specified by God to be Judge of the living and the dead. To this One are all the prophets testifying. Everyone who is believing on Him is to obtain the pardon of sins through His name.

As Peter is speaking the holy spirit falls on all those hearing the word. Those who accompany Peter are amazed, seeing that on the nations also the gratuity of the holy spirit has been poured out. Peter bids them to be baptized.

> To the Gentiles? Observe the shock on the part of the believing Jews (the ecclesia) that a Gentile would receive the holy spirit from God. It was hard for Peter to believe that he should even go to the house of a Gentile and proclaim the evangel to him.
>
> From the time of Abraham it was God's plan to *bless all peoples,* but until now God has worked strictly with the Jews. Jesus Himself would go only to the sheep of Israel, and "the church" (ecclesia) up to now is also exclusively

Jewish. Everything we have read thus far in Acts has pertained to the JEWISH believers. Has the plan now changed? Will God now go directly to the Gentiles?

Cornelius was no ordinary Gentile. He was devout, feared God, and beseeched God continually. He sought after the God of Abraham, and God now commissions Peter to go to him.

But as we read on, observe that Peter and the other apostles will continue to go exclusively to the Jews. We remember once again Paul's words; that Paul was entrusted with the evangel of the Uncircumcision, while Peter was entrusted with the evangel of the Circumcision. (Galatians 2:7)

CHAPTER 11

Peter criticized for going to the Gentiles (11:1)

Those of the Circumcision doubt Peter. *You entered to men having uncircumcision, and you ate with them.* Peter tells them of the vision he had received from God. *If, then, God gives them the equal gratuity as to us also, when believing on the Lord Jesus Christ, who was I – able to forbid God?*

They glorify God, saying, Consequently, to the nations also God gives repentance unto life.

Those who are dispersed evangelize (11:19)

Those who are dispersed evangelize as far as Phoenicia and Cyprus and Antioch, speaking the word to no one except TO THE JEWS ONLY. A vast number who believe turn back to the Lord.

> # To the JEWS only!

Note that they not only *believe*, but also *turn back to the Lord.* By inference we see that it is one thing to believe, and another to act (turn back). This is the message being proclaimed as a part of the "kingdom evangel" going to the Jews; to believe AND to repent (turn back).

Barnabas and Saul go to Antioch (11:22)

The ecclesia in Jerusalem delegates Barnabas to Antioch. He entreats them all with purpose of heart to be remaining in the Lord. Barnabas goes to

Tarsus to find Saul, and he brings him to Antioch. They remain there for a year with the ecclesia, teaching a considerable throng.

Agabus (a prophet) signifies thru the spirit the great famine which is about to be on the whole inhabited earth, which occurred under Claudius. As any of the disciples thrive, each of them designate something to send to the brethren dwelling in Judea, for dispensing.

The famine took place during the reign of Claudius, who reigned from 41-54 A.D.

CHAPTER 12

Major persecution (12:1)

Herod the king puts forth his hands to mistreat some from the ecclesia. He assassinates James, the brother of John. Peter is arrested and jailed.

Peter's release from prison (12:5)

The ecclesia earnestly pray for Peter. A messenger frees Peter from his chains and opens the gates. Peter tells them how *the Lord* let him out of jail. He goes from Judea into Caesarea.

Herod's death (12:20)

The people would say of Herod, A god's voice, and not a man's. A messenger of the Lord smites Herod because he gives not the glory to God.

The word of God grows (12:24)

Barnabas and Saul return from Jerusalem to Antioch, taking along John Mark.

PAUSE!

To this point the believers from among Israel, led by Peter and James, are central to the history recorded in Acts. Luke seems to be the author of Acts, addressing Theophilus in both accounts (compare Luke 1:3 with Acts 1:1). Acts is a continuation of Luke's gospel.

Israel once more hears the evangel of the kingdom, but now that message is strengthened by the resurrection of the King who had been crucified. Israel had rejected the kingdom during Jesus' earthly ministry as recorded in the gospel accounts. In Acts the holy spirit descends and the same kingdom message is again proclaimed; but it is rejected once again. The kingdom had been *locked* during Jesus' earthly ministry, and the keys were given to Peter. In Acts Peter unlocks the kingdom and it is once again proclaimed to Israel. But, sadly, once again it is rejected.

Acts is a transition. From this point forward we will see a change. Saul (Paul) will now become primary.

Remember that early in Acts, when Judas was replaced, it was important to keep the number of apostles at twelve. This makes sense since the apostles represented the ecclesia (called-out-ones) from among Israel which was comprised of twelve tribes.

But when Paul assumes the forefront and is named an apostle, this is a new thing. It will be twelve PLUS Paul. This makes sense since Paul is named apostle to the nations. This, too, is a new thing. To this point the nations are only blessed thru Israel. But later, in Paul's writings, we will see that the believers among the nations will be joint heirs, on the same level as Israel.

It is important to *rightly divide* the word of God, not mixing together things that are different. Doing so leads to confusion and a failure to understand that which God is trying to reveal to us.

The Twelve, and the early church (called-out-ones) recorded thus far in Acts are exclusively believers among Israel. We within the Body of Christ today cannot reach back and claim that the events recorded and the words spoken pertain to us today; for this was a time when God was working thru ISRAEL as His channel to bless all people.

With Paul, and especially with his later letters, we will see truths not revealed by the prophets, in the four gospel accounts, or in this first part of Acts.

And so we will pause here with our overview of Acts to look at the letters written by the leaders in Israel; letters written TO THE BELIEVERS AMONG ISRAEL. Once we have done this we will return to our study of Acts.

Acts
Part One: Peter

Post-Resurrection Appearances   1:1
- Art Thou at this time restoring the kingdom to Israel? (1:6)
- Not yours to know times or eras (1:7)
- *[Did not dispute kingdom was to be restored to Israel – only the timing.]*
- You will be my witnesses in Jerusalem, Judea & Samaria ... as far as the limits of the earth (1:8)

Judas Replaced   1:15
- To become a witness of His resurrection together with us (1:22)
- They chose only one to replace Judas ... retaining their number at Twelve

Pentecost   2:1
- "In Jerusalem, Jews, pious men from every nation" (2:5)
- "Men, Israelites! Hear these words..." (2:22)
- "Let all the house of Israel know ... that God makes Him Lord as well as Christ (2:36)
- "Repent and be baptized ... in the name of Jesus Christ ... for the pardon of your sins" (2:38)
- **About 3000 souls added in that day (2:41)**

Healing   3:1
- [Signs and wonders accompany the kingdom evangel, as in Matthew]

Peter's speech   3:11
- "Men! Israelites!" (3:11)
- "**Repent**, then, and turn about for the erasure of your sins,
- So that **seasons of refreshing** should be coming from the face of the Lord
- And He should **dispatch the One** fixed upon before for you, Christ Jesus
- Whom heaven must indeed receive until the times of restoration of all
- To you first God commissions Him to bless you by turning you from your wickedness (3:26)
- *[Much like, "Repent the kingdom is near"]*
- **Many hear and believe ... the number of men became about 5000 (4:4)**
- "Let it be known to you and to the entire people of Israel" (4:10)

The crucifixion designated by God   4:27
- Herod and Pontius Pilate, together with the nations and the peoples of Israel ... do whatever Thy hand and Thy counsel designates beforehand to occur

Miraculous events   5:1
- Immediate judgment on Ananias & Sapphira ... death (5:1)
- Many signs and miracles through the hands of the apostles (5:12)

Before the Sanhedrin   5:27
- The God of our fathers rouses Jesus on Whom you lay hands, hanging Him on a pole (5:30)
- God exalts to His right hand, to give repentance to Israel and the pardon of sins (5:31)

Dissension & Persecution   6:1
- Dissension arises between the Hellenists & Hebrews in the ecclesia (6)
- Stephen is stoned (7)
- Great persecution in Jerusalem ... dispersion in Judea & Samaria (8)
- The dispersed "evangelize" with the word (8:4)
- Philip brings "**the evangel concerning the kingdom of God** & the name of Jesus Christ" (8:12)

Saul's Conversion   9:1
- A choice instrument of Mine, to bear my name before both the ***nations and kings***, _besides_ the **sons of Israel** (9:15)
- Immediately, in the synagogues, he heralded Jesus, that He is the Son of God (9:20)

The ecclesia enjoys peace   9:31
- The ecclesia in all of Judea, Galilee and Samaria had peace, being edified... (9:31)
- **Their number "multiplied" (9:31)**
- Paralytic healed ... Tabitha raised from the dead (9:36)

Cornelius   10:1
- "Devout and fearing God ... doing many alms to the people and beseeching God continually"
- Peter: "I am grasping that God is not partial but in every nation he who is fearing Him and acting righteously is acceptable to Him" (10:35)

Continuing to go to Jews only 11:19
- Speaking the word to no one except to Jews only (11:19)

Major persecution 12:1
- James, brother of John, is assassinated by Herod (12:1)
- Peter arrested and jailed (12:3)
- Peter miraculously released by a messenger (12:5)
- A messenger of the Lord kills Herod (12:20)

Growth 12:24
- The word of God grows and was multiplied (12:24)

The Circumcision Letters

An Overview of the Scriptures, by
BOB EVELY © *2018.*
An Independent Minister of Christ Jesus,
Of the church at Wilmore, Kentucky

The epistles (or letters) we find in the Holy Scriptures can be divided into two categories:

- ✓ The Circumcision letters (those directed to Israel)
- ✓ The Uncircumcision letters (those written by Paul and directed to the Body of Christ; Jew and Gentile alike)

Consider what we have read in Acts. At first the Jewish leaders had difficulty with Paul since the evangel he proclaimed was so different. Where was the mention of the law in Paul's preaching? This conflict is recorded at length in Paul's letter to the Galatians.

The Judaizers challenged Paul at every turn, and insisted that the requirements of the law be ADDED to Paul's message. (Acts 15:1) But Paul was adamant that this NOT be done. For if the law was mixed with the evangel entrusted to him, it would become a DIFFERENT EVANGEL, a DISTORTION of his evangel. (Galatians 1:7)

So Paul is asked to appear before the Jerusalem council. (Acts 15:6) And there the Jewish leaders recognize that the evangel entrusted to Paul is DIFFERENT from the Circumcision evangel entrusted to Peter. (Galatians 2:6-9) As they part, James, Cephas (Peter) and John give Paul the right hand of fellowship. (Galatians 2:9)

As we study the Circumcision letters we must remember that Paul did not just take the same message to another people group (i.e. the nations). His message was DIFFERENT. So as we review the Circumcision letters keep in mind that the message contained in them is specific to ISRAEL, and in that particular era. Our specific message will be found in Paul's writings which we will take up later. Some general truths can be found, but as for attempting to directly apply specifics from these Circumcision letters in our present day within the Body of Christ ... BEWARE!

We must *correctly cut,* or *rightly divide,* the word of truth. (2 Timothy 2:15)

The Circumcision letters are an extension of the kingdom message operative in the first part of Acts, which bears the same message as that proclaimed during Jesus' earthly ministry. *The kingdom is near. Ready yourselves for the kingdom.* The message is concerned with Israel, upon the earth; whereas the message to the Body of Christ is concerned with all nations, with an expectation in the heavens. Any attempt to mix the messages found within the Circumcision letters with the messages proclaimed to the nations within Paul's writings will only lead to confusion, and a distortion of the message God has for us today.

The letters

Circumcision	Uncircumcision	
James		45 AD
Jude		46 AD
	1 Thessalonians	50-52 AD
	2 Thessalonians	52-53 AD
Hebrews		53-54 AD
	Galatians (early theory)	54 AD
1/2/3 John		55-56 AD
	1 Corinthians	Spring 57 AD
	2 Corinthians	Fall 57 AD
	Galatians	Winter 57 AD
	Romans	Spring 58 AD
1 Peter		60 AD
2 Peter		61 AD
	Colossians	61-62 AD
	Ephesians	61-62 AD
	Philemon	62-63 AD
	Philippians	63 AD
	1 Timothy	67 AD
	Titus	67 AD
	2 Timothy	Spring 68 AD

Note: There is some disagreement over the dating of some letters. The above is, in the author's opinion, the best estimate.

Hebrews

An Overview of the Scriptures, by
BOB EVELY © *2018.*
An Independent Minister of Christ Jesus,
Of the church at Wilmore, Kentucky

Circumcision	Uncircumcision	
James		45 AD
Jude		46 AD
	1 Thessalonians	50-52 AD
	2 Thessalonians	52-53 AD
Hebrews		**53-54 AD**
	Galatians (early theory)	54 AD
1/2/3 John		55-56 AD
	1 Corinthians	Spring 57 AD
	2 Corinthians	Fall 57 AD
	Galatians	Winter 57 AD
	Romans	Spring 58 AD
1 Peter		60 AD
2 Peter		61 AD
	Colossians	61-62 AD
	Ephesians	61-62 AD
	Philemon	62-63 AD
	Philippians	63 AD
	1 Timothy	67 AD
	Titus	67 AD
	2 Timothy	Spring 68 AD

The letter to the Hebrews is unique in that there is no signature. It would be a mistake to conjecture the author's identity, as this omission may be inspired in itself. The title *Hebrews* is not a part of the inspired text, though according to Bullinger *To Hebrews* is found in most texts. But it is clear from the opening and throughout the entire work that this is clearly written to the *Hebrew* believers within the early ecclesia. And so we must caution ...

WARNING!

This letter is clearly directed to the Hebrew believers within the early ecclesia, and not to those of the nations or the Body of Christ. All Scripture is for our benefit, but not all Scripture is written directly to us in this present age. We must take great care not to force direct application of this writing into our present context. God clearly deals differently with different people groups (Israel versus non-Israel) and in different eras.

CHAPTER 1

God has spoken (1:1)

God has spoken in many ways in the past, but now He has spoken to us thru a Son, thru Whom He makes the eons, and Who is the brightness of His glory and the emblem [image] of His person.

> *He has spoken to US* refers to Israel. The writer also notes that God spoke to *the fathers in the prophets*. The prophets addressed Israel, and not the world at large. We must remember that the writer is a Hebrew and he is writing to Hebrews.

The Son is superior to the angels and is seated at the right hand of God.

> The writer's argument is supported by references quoted from Psalm 2, Psalm 45, Psalm 102, Psalm 104, Psalm 110 and 2 Samuel 7:14.

CHAPTER 2

Do not neglect (2:1)

We must give close attention. If there were consequences for disobedience to the word brought by angels, how can we escape if we neglect the word of salvation brought by the Lord and confirmed by eyewitnesses, signs and wonders?

All in subjection to Christ (2:5)

Unlike the angels, God puts all things in subjection under the Son's feet in the impending inhabited earth. But we do not yet see all things under Him. Jesus was made a little lower than the angels, but then crowned with glory.

Christ is of the nature of men (2:9)

He was made a little lower than the angels, and tasted death for everyone. As the children are flesh and blood, He took part in the same; that thru death He might destroy him that had the power of death; the Adversary; and to deliver those who were subjected to bondage, fearing death.

God's work is progressive. All things are subject to Christ, but we do not yet see all things under Him.

He did not take on the nature of angels, but of the seed of Abraham. Made like His brethren, he could be a merciful and faithful chief priest; to be a propitiatory shelter for the sins of the people. Suffering and undergoing trial, He is able to help those were are being tried.

"Chief priest" clearly shows us this is directed to Israel.

CHAPTER 3

He is superior to Moses (3:1)

Moses was faithful, but Christ was counted worthy of more glory than Moses. Moses was faithful as a servant, but Christ as a Son over His own house. And we are of this house, IF we retain the boldness and the expectation unto the end.

More on this later, but let us here observe that perseverance is a requirement for these Hebrew believers.

Don't fall into unbelief (3:7)

Do not harden your hearts, as did your fathers who wandered in the wilderness. They did not enter into God's rest. Do not fall into unbelief. Entreat yourselves. We have become partners of Christ if we hold to our confidence unto the end. The stubborn from among our fathers in the wilderness could not enter His rest because of unbelief.

CHAPTER 4

Hear the gospel and enter "the stopping" (4:1)

Our fathers heard the gospel, but it did not profit them as it was not mixed with faith. We also have heard the gospel, and we who believe are entering into the rest. God stopped His works on the seventh day, and it remains for some to be entering into His stopping. Our fathers did not enter because of their stubbornness, but God specified thru David that today is the day if you should not be hardening your hearts. A *sabbatism* is left for the people of God. We should endeavor to enter into this rest.

The "stopping" of old referred to the promised land, delayed 40 years while the Hebrews wandered in the wilderness. And upon entering they never fully entered all that had been allotted. This is contrasted with the *stopping* that lies ahead for faithful Israel, when the Messiah returns and when the kingdom is restored upon the earth, this time in fullness.

The word of God is living and operative (4:12)

The word of God is living and operative, and keen above any two-edged sword, and penetrating up to the parting of soul and spirit, both of the articulations and marrow, and is a judge of the sentiments and thoughts of the heart.

There is not a creature that is not apparent in its sight. All is naked and bare to the eyes of Him to Whom we are accountable.

A great chief priest (4:14)

Since we have a great chief priest who has passed thru the heavens, Jesus the Son of God, we may be holding to our profession. He was tried in all respects, like us, but He did not sin. Therefore we may be coming with boldness to the throne of grace, obtaining mercy and grace.

CHAPTER 5

As is true of a chief priest, Christ does not glorify Himself, but God. He is a priest according to the order of Melchizadek. He learned obedience thru suffering. And when *perfected*, He became the cause of *eonian salvation* to all obeying Him.

> Christ is a HIGHER chief priest; a PERFECTED chief priest. Those obeying will have salvation and life in the eon to come. But this does not preclude those who have forfeited life in that eon from being ultimately reconciled to God at the end of the eons, in accord with God's will that all men be saved. (1 Timothy 2:4)

Move on to maturity (5:11)

By now you should be teachers, but still have need of one to teach you the basics; milk, not solid food. We should be brought on to maturity, not again disrupting the foundations; repentance from dead works, faith, baptizings, the laying of hands, the resurrection of the dead, and eonian judgment.

> It would appear, then, that there were challenges and disputes over these basic teachings that were preventing the believers from moving on to maturity.

CHAPTER 6

Repentance cannot be renewed (6:4)

Once enlightened; tasting the celestial grace, the holy spirit, the ideal declarations of God, the powerful deeds of *the impending eon;* if one falls aside it is impossible to renew to repentance. But we are persuaded of better things concerning your salvation. God does not forget your work and the love that you display for His name when you serve the saints.

> We must remember that these were Hebrew believers, whose expectation was the return of the Messiah to restore the kingdom. In anticipation of this coming kingdom, perseverance was needed to be qualified. It is interesting that when the called-for repentance does not come, and the coming kingdom is delayed until the complement of the nations enters, (Romans 11:25) God works in a new direction not described in Hebrews. Thru Paul He will announce the Body of Christ, a heavenly expectation not upon this earth, where repentance and perseverance are not requirements. It will be fully the grace and the work of God, lest any man boast.
>
> But in this present context, to the Hebrew believers, perseverance is required, and if one falls back and rejects Christ they will be hardened and it will be impossible to renew to repentance. This one will have forfeited the enjoyment of his allotment in the eon to come, although he will not and cannot forfeit his ultimate reconciliation with God at the end of the ages.

Be diligent ^(6:11)

Be diligent, assured of the expectation until the end. Imitate the examples of faith and patience. Abraham was patient, and he happened upon the promise. God has promised the enjoyment of the allotment by an oath. We who flee for refuge have a strong consolation and a secure expectation that has been confirmed.

A chief priest in the order of Melchizadek ^(6:20)

Jesus became chief priest according to the order of Melchizadek, for the eon.

CHAPTER 7

Melchizadek was a different kind of priest. He was king of righteousness and king of peace. He had no geneology; no beginning or end. He pictured the Son of God, remaining a priest to a finality. If the Levitical priesthood was perfect, why would there be the need for a different priest according to the order of Melchizadek? The priesthood needed to be transferred, as the law also. Our Lord is of the tribe of Judah, not the tribe of priests. He is a priest for the eon according to the order of Melchizadek. The preceding precept is weak. The law does not perfect. We have a *better* expectation. This priest (Christ) comes thru an oath by God. He is the sponsor of a better covenant. The former priests all died, but this one remains for the eon. He is able to save to the uttermost those coming to God thru Him. Undefiled, separated from sinners, residing in the heavens; daily sacrifices are no longer necessary. He offered Himself once for all time.

CHAPTER 8

A better tabernacle and covenant ^(8:1)

Such is our chief priest, seated at the right hand of the throne. He is minister of the true tabernacle. The tabernacle of old was based on the model shown to Moses in the mountain. Christ is Mediator of a *better* covenant based on *better* promises. As promised, God's laws will be imparted *to their comprehension* and inscribed on their hearts. They will be acquainted with the Lord. God will not be reminded of their sins and lawlessnesses. The old covenant is near its disappearance.

> The Old Testament passages quoted by the writer remind us that the prophets announced a covenant with THE HOUSE OF ISRAEL AND THE HOUSE OF JUDAH; not the nations. Clearly this prophesy was not yet fulfilled. The hearers were being encouraged to repent and to persevere in view of the fulfillment of this new covenant. This was their expectation. It was not yet in place. This may be what Paul spoke of in Romans 11:25-27, referring to the day when all Israel will be saved.

CHAPTER 9

In the former tabernacle, priests performed divine service continually, but in the holy of holies only once a year, with blood. This is *a parable* for the present. Those were sacrifices that could not perfect as to conscience, but only *in foods and drinks and baptizings ... for the flesh.* But now comes Christ, and a *greater* tabernacle not made by hands. His own blood is a *better* sacrifice; once for all into the holy places, resulting in *eonian redemption.*

He is the Mediator of a new covenant, so that those under the first covenant may obtain the promise of *eonian* enjoyment of the allotment. And without blood there is no pardon.

> Here we see that the new covenant pertains to those who were under the old covenant; that is, ISRAEL.

A better sacrifice ^(9:23)

For the sake of the examples a *better* sacrifice was necessary. And celestial things required a *better* sacrifice. Christ has entered not holy places made by hands but the holy place in heaven. Once, *at the conclusion of the eons,* for the repudiation of sin through His sacrifice, is He manifest.

It is not that Christ died at the end of the eons. This would not make sense, as He has in fact died but we are not yet at the end of the eons. He is *manifest* at the end of the eons. To some He is manifest now, but at the end of the eons He will be *fully* manifest to all, and what He has accomplished will be understood by all.

CHAPTER 10

The old sacrifices could never perfect; they were never final. It was impossible for the blood of these sacrifices to eliminate sins. As was prophesied, God does not will or delight in sacrifices, but in the One to come Who would do His will. The first is ended to establish the second. We are hallowed thru Christ's sacrifice. The priests stood, offering daily sacrifices. Christ is seated. He is waiting until His enemies are at His feet. By one sacrifice He has perfected with finality those who are hallowed. With the new covenant there is pardon. There is no longer an approach present concerned with sin. So; we may be approaching with a true heart, in the assurance of faith; avowing the expectation without wavering; and inciting one another to love and ideal acts, not forsaking assembling together.

Not forsaking the assembling (10:25)

Not forsaking the assembling of ourselves, according as the custom of some is, but entreating, and so much rather as you are observing the day drawing near.

At this point the believers were exclusively those from among Israel. They were still meeting in synagogues. Assembling in specific places was always an important thing for Israel, and even commanded by God on the feast days. But we must remember that this passage is speaking to ISRAEL, and in this particular era. Later, in Paul's ministry to the nations, we see no command to assemble at specific places. Often the believers met in homes. There is no record, until later centuries, of believers from among the nations gathering at specific times or in specific places.

There is certainly much to be gained when we meet together. We can encourage one another, and entreat one another toward greater faith and good works. But for us within the Body of Christ in our present day there is no command or instruction to meet together at specific times or places. We can encourage one another within our families, our circle of friends, our work associates, and our neighborhoods.

Worship happens when we revere God, even when we are alone. "Corporate worship" is not commanded for the Body of Christ.

As a matter of fact, those assembling together with other believers within "organized churches" should beware. Much that happens within the life of organized churches is based on the traditions of men and not the word of God. Teachings are largely built on the traditions and teachings of men, and not the pure word of God. Much error is taught concerning the will of God.

Traditional churches can provide venues for believers to meet together, but take care not to become contaminated by the traditions of men; just as Jesus once warned those of Israel in the days of His earthly ministry.

Warning against voluntary sin (10:26)

After recognizing truth, if we sin voluntarily there is not a sacrifice concerning sins, but just a fearful waiting for judging; he who rejects the blood of the covenant that has hallowed him. *Mine is vengeance! I will repay! the Lord is saying.*

From the context, this voluntary sin appears to specifically refer to the sin of falling away from the faith; rejecting Christ's blood as the sacrifice. And remember, this pertains to the believers among Israel; and in that day.

Endure, and have faith (10:32)

Remember the former days when you suffered and were reproached, yet believed; knowing you have a better and a permanent property in the heavens. Have endurance. Do God's will. Christ is coming. The just shall be living by faith. We do not shrink back to destruction; we have faith that procures the soul.

Faith that procures the soul speaks of that which secures life in the eon to come, which would be forfeited if faith is rejected. Again, this speaks to the Hebrew believers who awaited the coming kingdom. Faith within the Body of Christ carries a different expectation, where perseverance is not demanded; since faith for the Body of Christ is *the faith of Christ;* fully of God; lest any should boast.

CHAPTER 11

Faith (11:1)

Faith is an assumption of what is being expected; a conviction concerning matters that are not being observed. By faith we are understanding that the eons are to *adjust* to God's declaration, so that what we observe *has not come out of what is appearing.*

> In other words, this new chief priest, new sacrifice, new covenant, new tabernacle, new Mediator; are all things requiring faith. They do not appear to be naturally following what the Hebrews had observed for centuries.

Examples of faith include Abel, Enoch, Noah, Abraham, Sarah. One coming to God *must believe that He is,* and that He is *becoming a Rewarder of those who are seeking Him out.*

> One coming to God is to believe in this fashion, even if the reward has not yet been realized and enjoyed.

All of these examples died not having received the things promised, but only seeing them still to come. They all craved a better future; celestial. Other examples of faith include Isaac, Jacob, Joseph, Moses, the fall of Jericho, Rahab, and others. None of these received the promise concerning us, and apart from us they are not perfected.

CHAPTER 12

Therefore ... endure (12:1)

Therefore; have endurance. Look to Jesus, the inaugurator and perfector of faith. Consider Him Who endured a cross, and contradiction by sinners.

The Lord's discipline (12:5)

Do not disdain the discipline of the Lord. The Lord disciplines those He loves. What son is not disciplined by his father? If we are not disciplined then we are not sons. He disciplines for our good; for us to partake of His holiness. Pursue peace with all; and holiness. Supervise, that none lack God's grace.

Esau's example (12:16)

Remember Esau gave up his birthright and was later rejected from enjoying the allotment.

> Esau forfeited the enjoyment of what would have been his to enjoy. But he did not experience eternal torment as a result. It was a loss of reward that he experienced. We must remember that to forfeit the enjoyment of the allotment is a loss of reward, but does not signify eternal torment as many within the churches of man teach.

You have grace; do not refuse Him (12:18)

You have come to mount Zion, celestial Jerusalem; to Jesus, Mediator of a fresh covenant. Beware. Do not refuse Him. How can we escape if we do? We may have grace and offer divine service pleasing to God, with piety and dread, for our God is also a consuming fire.

> Full and complete grace, as proclaimed by Paul, is not yet seen here. There is grace, but always the need for perseverance lest one falls and becomes disqualified, and subject to the consuming fire. But even here, the consuming fire is not an eternal torment. It will last only to the end of the eons, serving the purpose of bringing all of creation into subjection and reconciliation.

CHAPTER 13

Closing instructions regarding behavior (13:1)

Exhibit brotherly fondness. Be mindful of those bound and mistreated. Keep marriage pure. Do not be fond of money; be content. Remember your leaders who speak the word of God to you. Imitate their faith. Be not carried away by strange teachings, for we have an altar they have no right to.

> Since the altar is one they have no right to, this would seem to imply that the strange teachings are coming from pagan religions. Much of this letter is a warning against falling back to Judaism, at the encouragement of the non-believing Hebrews. But this warning against strange teachings seems to be different; a warning against the following of strange teachings of the pagan nations, and probably including Gnosticism which was prevalent in this day.

We bear reproach as He did. Here we do not have a permanent city, but seek the one that is coming. Offer sacrifices of praise continually. Do well, and contribute. Heed your leaders and defer to them. Pray concerning us. May God adapt you to every good work, to do His will.

Bear these words of entreaty (13:22)

> With this admonition repeated once again as the letter concludes, we see that the primary purpose of this writing is to entreat the Hebrew believers to *persevere* in their faith; not falling back to Judaism as they were being tempted to do.

SUMMARY

In the past God spoke in a variety of ways, but now He has spoken thru a Son; Who is superior to angels and to Moses. God puts all in subjection to Christ, though we do not yet see this. Christ is a great chief priest. We have a better tabernacle, covenant, and sacrifice. The Lord disciplines those He loves.

The letter's recipients were instructed to lay hold of the expectation lying before them. (6:18) But what was their expectation? The promise of the eonian enjoyment of the allotment. (9:15) That is; life in the eon to come when Christ comes *a second time*. (9:28) God's laws would be imparted to their hearts; inscribed on their comprehensions. (10:16-17) Being made ready for them was an unshakable kingdom. (12:28) At present they did not have a permanent city, but were seeking for the one which is impending. (13:14)

And what were the entreaties made by the writer to those living in that day? To give close attention to the word of salvation, and not to fall into unbelief. To move on to maturity. To be diligent. To endure and have faith, drawing strength from the examples of faith and patience in those that preceded them. To exhibit behavior that was fitting: Brotherly fondness, being mindful of those bound and mistreated, keeping marriage pure, not being fond of money, being content, remembering their leaders who spoke the word of God to them, not to be carried away by strange teachings, to offer praise continually, to do well and contribute, to heed their leaders, and to pray concerning the writer. To bear the words of the entreaty being made.

Clearly the Hebrew believers were facing a crisis, and many were falling away. Perhaps this was because the signs and wonders had ceased, or at least slowed. Perhaps it was because of the influence of the Hellenists; the sheep of Israel that had lived in foreign lands and adopted Greek culture, customs and beliefs concerning God. Whatever the case, the purpose of this letter seems to be to encourage the believers not to fall away in these difficult times, but to adhere to their faith; strengthened by the example of those that had preceded them.

James

An Overview of the Scriptures, by
BOB EVELY © *2018.*
An Independent Minister of Christ Jesus,
Of the church at Wilmore, Kentucky

Circumcision	Uncircumcision	
James		45 AD
Jude		46 AD
	1 Thessalonians	50-52 AD
	2 Thessalonians	52-53 AD
Hebrews		53-54 AD
	Galatians (early theory)	54 AD
1/2/3 John		55-56 AD
	1 Corinthians	Spring 57 AD
	2 Corinthians	Fall 57 AD
	Galatians	Winter 57 AD
	Romans	Spring 58 AD
1 Peter		60 AD
2 Peter		61 AD
	Colossians	61-62 AD
	Ephesians	61-62 AD
	Philemon	62-63 AD
	Philippians	63 AD
	1 Timothy	67 AD
	Titus	67 AD
	2 Timothy	Spring 68 AD

James was the brother of Jesus. (Matthew 13:55; Mark 6:3) When James is mentioned in Acts 12:17 it is clear he is not the apostle James, for the latter had been killed in Acts 12:2.

James lived in the land of Israel his entire life. In the early part of Acts, Peter is chief among the apostles and was foremost in proclaiming the Circumcision evangel. But as early as Paul's first visit to Jerusalem, James had a prominent place though he was not an apostle. (Galatians 1:19) Fourteen years later he had risen to become one of the *pillars* in Jerusalem and was named before Peter and John. (Galatians 2:9) Peter became concerned about the teachings of those associated with James. (Galatians 2:12) At the council in Jerusalem to consider the question of requiring those of the nations to be circumcised, James had the decisive word which placed requirements on the nations. (Colossians 2:14) The decree was later nullified as the secret administration was revealed thru Paul. (Ephesians 2:15) It would seem that as the apostasy increased within the ecclesia and as greater emphasis was placed upon the physical connection to the Lord, James rose in prominence. But Paul repudiates any physical connection to the Lord. (Philippians 3:4-12)

E. W. Bullinger, in *How to Enjoy the Bible,* notes that James' epistle is filled with references to the Sermon on the Mount; also directed specifically to Israel. In fact, Bullinger cites 25 passages in James that relate directly to the Sermon on the Mount.

CHAPTER 1

The address on the envelope (1:1)

James identifies himself as the author and directs the letter *to the* TWELVE TRIBES *in the dispersion.*

> If my father were to direct a letter to my brother, I could learn from what is written, but I could not claim any of the specifics as if it were written to me. When James writes to the twelve tribes who were dispersed because of persecution, we must remember that these are BELIEVERS FROM AMONG ISRAEL. Yes, there may be general principles that can be observed, but the specifics were written TO ISRAEL and not to the Body of Christ. We begin with this caution ...

WARNING!

> This letter is directed to the believing "sheep of Israel" within the early ecclesia, and not to the Body of Christ. All Scripture is for our benefit, but not all Scripture is written directly TO us in this present age. We must take great care not to force direct application of all elements in this writing into our present context. God clearly deals differently with different people groups (Israel versus non-Israel) and in different eras.

Trials have a purpose (1:2)

When falling into trials the brethren can rejoice, because the testing of one's faith produces endurance, and endurance will cause one to be *perfect and unimpaired,* lacking in nothing.

> Here we see the purpose of this letter, at least in part. The dispersed of Israel faced trials and needed encouragement.

Ask for wisdom without doubting (1:5)

The one lacking wisdom should request it from God with faith. God gives generously to all, and if wisdom is requested it will be given. But the request must be made in faith, doubting nothing. One who doubts is tossed as the wind surges the sea. He is double-souled and turbulent in all his ways, and he shall not be obtaining anything from the Lord.

> Again we remind the reader that these instructions were given to Israel, and specifically in that day. How can we make the assumption that this directive pertains to we who are Gentiles, or even to those of Israel in this present day? Consider Paul's request for the thorn in his flesh to be removed. (2 Corinthians 12:7-10) It was not removed. Did Paul not ask in faith? It is more likely that the era had passed, and God is now acting in a different way. Grace is sufficient, and infirmities demonstrate God's power.

Be humble (1:9)

Riches will fade. The humble brother should glory in his exaltation, and the rich in his humiliation, for the rich shall be caused to fade.

Enduring trials (1:12)

Happy is the man enduring trial, for trial will qualify him and he will obtain the wreath of life. Trials do not come from God, for God tries no one. Trial comes when one is lured by his own desire, and when desire conceives it brings forth sin, which in turn brings forth death. All good giving and every perfect gratuity is from above, descending from the Father of lights, in Whom there is no mutation or shadow from revolving motion.

Firstfruit (1:18)

By intention, He teems forth us by the word of truth, for us to be some *firstfruit* of His own creatures.

> This is why enduring trials, while the world looks on, is important. Believing Israel is the FIRSTFRUIT of God's creatures. That is, they are not the *only* ones to be God's creatures, but the *firstfruit,* as more are to follow.

Meekness, not anger (1:19)

The brethren are to be swift to hear but slow to speak, and slow to anger. Anger is not working the righteousness of God. Put off filthiness and evil, and receive with meekness the implanted word, which is able to *save your souls.*

> The soul is the consciousness aspect of man. It is what gives us sensations. When God's spirit animated the soil, Adam was given life. Upon death, the soil returns to the soil, the spirit returns to God who gave it, and our soul goes to hades, or the unseen realm. There is no consciousness. There is no life. The soul, therefore, is conscious life. For one's soul to be saved could refer to having conscious life in this present age (the life we currently experience), but most often in the Scriptures it refers to having conscious life in the age to come. Those whose souls have been saved will enjoy conscious life in the age to come, while those not saved will not. But in either case, ALL will ultimately experience life, for God is the Saviour of ALL, and this will be fully realized at the consummation when God becomes All in all. (1 Corinthians 15:28)

Doers of the word (1:22)

Become doers of the word, and not only listeners, beguiling yourselves. The one who is a doer of the word will be happy in his doing. If one is a ritualist, not bridling his tongue, his ritual is in vain because a clean and undefiled ritual is to visit the bereaved and widowed in their affliction, and to keep oneself unspotted from the world.

> We see the contrast between the word and the world; and between ritualistic words and deeds.

CHAPTER 2

Don't favor the rich (2:1)

If one who is obviously rich enters your *synagogue* and one who is obviously poor, do not show preference by seating the rich and asking the poor to stand. God chose the poor in the world, as they were rich in faith and they enjoy the allotment of the kingdom. Yet you dishonor the poor, while the rich tyrannize you and draw you to tribunals as they blaspheme. If you discharge the royal law, according to the scripture, you shall be loving your associate as yourself, and you will be doing ideally. But if you show partiality you are transgressors, working sin. For anyone *keeping the whole law* yet tripping in one thing, he has become liable for all. Judging is merciless to him who does not exercise mercy.

> The reference to *your synagogue* reiterates that James' audience is believing ISRAEL. And observe the reference to *keeping the whole law;* also pertaining to Israel.

Works needed for salvation (2:14)

If one proclaims faith but has no works, that faith cannot save him. If a brother or sister needs food or clothing, yet you tell them to go in peace without giving them food or clothing, what is the benefit? Faith, if it should not have works: it is dead by itself. Show me your faith apart from the works and I shall be showing you my faith by my works. You believe that God is one, but the demons also believe and are shuddering.

Abraham's example (2:21)

Was Abraham not justified by works when offering up his son Isaac on the altar? Faith worked together with his works, and by works was faith perfected. And fulfilled was the scripture which is saying, Now Abraham believes God, and it is reckoned to him for righteousness.

JUSTIFICATION IS NOT BY FAITH ALONE (2:24)

You see that by works a man is being justified, and not by faith alone.

> ## This is an astonishing statement!

This statement directly conflicts with Paul's claim in Romans. *For we are reckoning a man to be justified by faith apart from works of law.* (Romans 3:28) *For if Abraham was justified by acts, he has something to boast in ... Abraham believes God, and it is reckoned to him for righteousness. Now to the worker, the wage is not reckoned as a favor, but as a debt. Yet to him who is not working yet is believing on Him ... his faith is reckoned for righteousness.* (Romans 4:1-15)

Interestingly, James uses an example from Abraham's life as found in Genesis 22, AFTER he was circumcised and illustrating Abraham's obedience. In Romans 3, Paul uses an example found in Genesis 15 BEFORE Abraham's circumcision that was to do with his spiritual seed, apart from any works.

In Matthew, as Jesus proclaimed the coming kingdom to be restored upon the earth, works is crucial to entrance into the kingdom. In the Circumcision letters (James being one of them) we see the salvation requirement of faith plus works, for the audience (believing Israel) was still being prepared for entry into the kingdom to come upon the earth. But Paul's evangel was different. He received it directly from the Lord. It was the next step in God's progressive revelation, and works no longer played a part.

Consider the progression. In the Old Testament the requirement was works. For believing Israel the requirement is faith plus works. In both cases the recipients of the word displayed inability in meeting the requirement. Who, then, can be saved? All this to take humanity to the place where it is recognized that only God's grace can save. Paul proclaimed faith, with no works requirement. Yes, ideal acts were called for as a <u>response</u> to God's grace, but not as a <u>requirement</u> for salvation. One without works would be saved, yet as one escaping through fire. (1 Corinthians 3:15)

So we see the importance of recognizing the distinction between the Circumcision evangel, as proclaimed here by James, and the Uncircumcision evangel as proclaimed by Paul. Any who attempt to mix the two messages will be distorting the evangel and preaching A DIFFERENT EVANGEL, as Paul warned of in Galatians 1:6-9. And the difficulty in reconciling James 2:24 with Romans 3:28 may cause us to discount one or the other, as did Martin Luther who considered James to be an "epistle of straw" and not worthy of being considered Scripture.

<u>Rahab's example</u> (2:25)

Rahab the prostitute was justified by works when entertaining the messengers and preserving them by sending them out a different way. For even as the body apart from spirit is dead, thus also faith apart from works is dead.

This could be the key to understanding the difference between James and Paul. Israel was promised regeneration, but the Body of Christ is a new creation. Paul proclaimed that the Body of Christ believers have died with Christ. No longer in body, they were now reckoned as spirit; a new creation. While the fullness of this fact will not be realized until the resurrection, God *reckons* the body in this way even at present. Our old creation is gone. We now live in Christ.

So Israel awaits regeneration and will serve the Lord upon the earth, and entrance into the kingdom will require faith plus works. But the Body of Christ is reckoned dead and a new creation, and upon resurrection will serve the Lord in the celestial realm. And even today, reckoning our old self dead and now living in Christ, the requirement is faith alone.

CHAPTER 3

A warning to teachers (3:1)

Not many should become teachers, as they will be getting greater judgment, for they are tripping much. Any who are not tripping in word is a perfect man, able to bridle the whole body also.

The tongue (3:3)

A horse is controlled by a small bit. A ship is controlled by a small rudder. So also the tongue is a small member, but controls the entire body. It can steer us to Gehenna.

> Not hell, as in some translations, but the *Valley of Hinnom* which was a dumping ground outside Jersusalem where fires burned continually, and where in the eons to come the bodies of the wicked will be cast.

While man has successfully tamed creatures of various kinds, no man can tame the tongue. With it we bless the Lord and Father, and with it we curse men who are in Gods likeness. But there is no need for it to become thus. No well can spring forth the sweet and bitter. No fig tree can produce olives. *Let the wise show ideal behavior, meekness and wisdom.*

Jealousy and faction (3:14)

If you have bitter jealousy and faction in your heart, are you not working against and falsifying the truth? This is not wisdom coming down from above, but terrestrial, soulish and demoniacal. Wherever there is jealousy and faction, there is turbulence and bad practice.

Wisdom from above (3:17)

The wisdom from above is pure, peaceable, lenient, compliant, bulging with mercy and good fruits, undiscriminating, unfeigned. The fruit of righteousness is being sown in peace.

CHAPTER 4

Battles and fighting (4:1)

Battles and fighting among you come from your gratifications warring in your members. You covet and cannot have. You murder and are jealous. You fight and battle and you have not. You request and cannot obtain, because you request evilly so as to spend it on your gratifications. You are adulterers and adulteresses.

> We see from this letter that the believers were being influenced by the temptations of the flesh; fighting, jealousy, faction, fleshly gratifications, and

coveting. James encourages them to remain focused on spiritual things; ideal behavior, meekness, and wisdom.

The humble receive grace (4:4)

Are you not aware that friendship of this world is enmity with God? If you seek to be a friend of the world, you are constituted an enemy of God. Does the spirit dwelling in us long to envy? But the grace He is giving is greater. God resists the proud, but He gives grace to the humble.

Resist the Adversary (4:7)

You may be subject, then, to God, yet withstand the Adversary, and he will be fleeing from you. Draw near to God, and He will be drawing near to you. Cleanse your hands, purify your hearts. Mourn, lament and be dejected. Be humbled, then, in the Lord's sight, and He shall be exalting you.

Don't speak evil against a brother (4:11)

Don't speak evil against a brother or judge a brother, for in doing so you speak against law and judge law. You therefore become a judge of law, not a doer of law. One is both Lawgiver and Judge, Who can save or destroy. Who are you to judge an associate?

Don't presume to know the future (4:13)

You say "Today or tomorrow we will be going here or there, spending a year there." But you are not versed as to tomorrow. You are a vapor, appearing briefly and then disappearing. Instead say, "If the Lord should be willing, and if we shall be living, then we will do this or that."

Boasting (4:16)

You are vaunting in your ostentations. Your boasting is wicked. When one perceives how to do the ideal but is not doing it, to him it is sin.

CHAPTER 5

The rich should lament (5:1)

The rich should lament, howling for the wretchedness to come. Your riches have rotted. Your gold and silver corrode and will give testimony against you. You hoard in the last days. You withhold wages from your workers, and their imploring has entered the ears of the Lord. You luxuriate on the earth and squander. You convict and murder the just who do not resist you. Be patient, then, brethren, till the presence of the Lord. Be patient; establish your hearts, for the presence of the Lord is near.

Don't groan against one another (5:9)

Don't groan against one another lest you be judged. The Judge stands before the doors.

Endure the evil (5:10)

The prophets who speak in the name of the Lord are your example for suffering evil and having patience. Happy are those who endure. You hear of the endurance of Job, and you see the consummation of the Lord, for He is compassionate and pitiful.

No oaths (5:12)

Do not swear, neither by heaven or earth, nor any other oath. Let your yes be yes, and your no be no, lest you fall under judging.

A word to those suffering and infirm (5:13)

If you suffer evil, pray. If you are cheerful, play music. If you are infirm, call the elders of the ecclesia to pray over you, applying oil in the name of the Lord. And the vow of faith will be saving the faltering; the Lord will raise him up, and if he has sinned it will be forgiven. Then confess sins to one another and pray for one another, so that you may be healed.

Pray (5:16)

The operative petition of the just is availing much. Elijah prayed for it not to rain, and it did not rain. He prayed for rain, and heaven gives a shower.

Turn back those who have strayed (5:19)

If any have been led astray from the truth, the one turning him back will be saving his soul from death and will be covering a multitude of sins.

SUMMARY

From this letter we can develop a picture of the situation the believers faced. They were experiencing trials. James reminds them that trials have a purpose, testing faith and producing endurance. Trials do not come from God. They come when one is lured by his own desire, bringing forth sin and, in turn, death.

They were lacking in wisdom, and James counsels that they should request it from God, with faith.

Preference was being granted to the rich. But riches will fade. The rich should beware. Gold and silver corrode and will give testimony against them.

They were lacking in good acts and behavior. But if one proclaims faith but has no works, that faith cannot save him. By works a man is being justified, and not by faith alone. They were to be doers of the word and not just listeners only.

There was jealousy and factions, fighting, self-gratification, pride, speaking evil of the brethren and boasting. James entreats them to show ideal behavior, meekness and wisdom. They should not have jealousy and faction in their hearts. Wisdom from above is pure, peaceable, lenient, compliant, merciful, undiscriminating and unfeigned. Battles and fighting come from their gratifications. God resists the proud and gives grace to the humble. James entreats them to be humble; swift to hear, slow to speak and slow to anger.

Some were suffering evil and were encouraged to endure. They were instructed to endure evil.

They were speaking evil against one another. James instructs them not to do so, or to judge a brother, or to groan against one another. They should beware of the tongue; for it can bless but also curse. It is small but controls the entire body, and can lead one to Gehenna.

The Adversary was at work, and James entreats them to resist the Adversary. Be subject to God.

They should not presume to know the future. Life is a vapor. Boasting is wicked. They should not swear oaths. They should pray, and turn back those who had strayed.

WARNING!

Once again we must be reminded; James' audience is ISRAEL and not the nations. We can observe some general principles; but must take care not to directly apply specifics. This letter was directed to believing ISRAEL, and in a past era. If we try to apply specifics, we will find irreconcilable conflicts with the specifics directed to the Body of Christ in Paul's writings (e.g. faith alone vs. faith plus works).

1 Peter

An Overview of the Scriptures, by
BOB EVELY © *2018.*
An Independent Minister of Christ Jesus,
Of the church at Wilmore, Kentucky

Circumcision	Uncircumcision	
James		45 AD
Jude		46 AD
	1 Thessalonians	50-52 AD
	2 Thessalonians	52-53 AD
Hebrews		53-54 AD
	Galatians (early theory)	54 AD
1/2/3 John		55-56 AD
	1 Corinthians	Spring 57 AD
	2 Corinthians	Fall 57 AD
	Galatians	Winter 57 AD
	Romans	Spring 58 AD
1 Peter		**60 AD**
2 Peter		61 AD
	Colossians	61-62 AD
	Ephesians	61-62 AD
	Philemon	62-63 AD
	Philippians	63 AD
	1 Timothy	67 AD
	Titus	67 AD
	2 Timothy	Spring 68 AD

Peter identifies himself as the writer of this letter. (1:1) Peter was chief among the twelve apostles throughout Jesus' earthly ministry, and we recall that the ministry of the apostles was directed *exclusively to the sheep of Israel.* (Matthew 10:6;15:24) Even after Christ's resurrection Peter addressed only *the house of Israel.* (Acts 2:14-36) In Acts we see Peter as the foundation on which the Circumcision ecclesia (believers from among Israel) was built. He remained chief of the twelve until superseded by the Lord's brother James in the Pentecostal era.

Peter was given the keys to the kingdom, (Matthew 16:19) and it was the kingdom to be restored unto Israel upon the earth that he proclaimed. Baptism and repentance continually accompanied the proclamation of the kingdom, or the Circumcision evangel.

Paul tells us that he had been entrusted with the *evangel of the Uncircumcision,* and Peter had been entrusted with the *evangel of the Circumcision.* (Galatians 2:7) He did not say that his was the evangel TO the Uncircumcision; but OF the Uncircumcision. It was A DIFFERENT MESSAGE, and this can be clearly seen if we examine the details. Whereas Paul addressed the ecclesia (church) which is Christ's Body, Peter writes to *a chosen race, a royal priesthood, a holy nation.*

WARNING!

Peter's letter is directed to the believing "sheep of Israel" within the early ecclesia, and not to the Body of Christ. All Scripture is for our benefit, but not all Scripture is written directly *to* us in this present age. We must take great care not to force direct application of all elements in this writing into our present context. God clearly deals differently with different people groups (Israel versus non-Israel) and in different eras.

We must *correctly cut,* or *rightly divide,* the word of truth. (2 Timothy 2:15)

In contrast to Paul who was a persecutor of Christ and of believers, Peter was a devout and obedient Israelite. He wrote *to the chosen expatriates of the dispersion of Pontus, Galatia, Cappadocia, the province of Asia, and Bithynia* (1 Peter 1:1) This clearly ties Peter's writings to the Circumcision (Israel), as the Gentiles were never dispersed to Asia Minor from their own land. It was the Jewish Christians that were forced to flee at the time of Stephen's stoning.

Believing Israel finds itself in the midst of persecution and suffering, probably during the reign of Nero when Christians were tortured and killed routinely. Peter's writings have no direct application for us in this era, as Paul's evangel of the Uncircumcision and his revelations of the mysteries previously hidden now pertain. But Peter's epistles will be a great comfort to those among Israel facing terrible persecutions in the days preceding the Lord's return to restore the kingdom; which we read of in Revelation.

Believing the Lord's return was near, Peter wrote to encourage them as they endured suffering, pointing to the expectation that lay before them. And he encouraged them to persevere and remain obedient, living holy (set apart) lives, exhibiting behavior in contrast to that of the nations.

Peter's commission to write his epistles came from the Lord after His ascension, when Peter was instructed to graze His lambkins and to tend His sheep. (John 21:15-17)

CHAPTER 1

The address on the envelope (1:1)

From Peter ...
To the chosen expatriates of the dispersion.

> The *chosen expatriates of the dispersion of Pontus, Galatia, Cappadocia, the province of Asia, and Bithynia* clearly refer to the Circumcision (Israel), as those of the nations were never dispersed from their own land to Asia Minor. It was the <u>Jewish</u> believers that were forced to disperse in the persecution that followed the stoning of Stephen.

The expectation of believing Israel (1:3)

God *regenerates* us and gives us *a living expectation through the resurrection of Jesus Christ, for the enjoyment of an allotment incorruptible, kept in the heavens for you ... for salvation ready to be revealed in the last era.*

> Their salvation is not yet realized. It will be revealed in the last era. But they can enjoy their coming allotment with *expectation* as it is being kept for them incorruptible.

> Israel's expectation was never to "go to heaven" when resurrected, but was instead to enjoy life upon the earth when Christ returns and reigns. Their expectation is *kept* in the heavens, but their destiny is not to *live* in the heavens. Consider the new earth that will descend <u>from out of the heavens</u>, but is not heaven itself. (Revelation 21:2) The notion that all die and go to heaven (or hell) at the time of death comes from TRADITION and not Scriptural REVELATION. In fact, the Body of Christ is destined to meet the Lord in the air and to serve Him in the heavenly realms at the resurrection, (1 Thessalonians 4:13ff) but the destiny of believing Israel to whom Peter writes is to serve the Lord upon the earth, and then subsequently the new earth, following their resurrection.

As you face trials and testing ^(1:6)

In which you are exulting; briefly at present, if it must be, being sorrowed by various trials, that the testing of your faith, much more precious than gold which is perishing, yet, being tested by fire, may be found for applause and glory and honor at the unveiling of Jesus Christ ...

> Peter reminds believing Israel that they only exult briefly as they consider their *expectation*, while enduring the harsh day-to-day reality of a life filled with testing and suffering. But at the unveiling of Jesus Christ (i.e. at His return) they will exult fully.
>
> The phrase, *The unveiling of Jesus Christ* (1:8) also opens the last book of the Bible, commonly called Revelation, which speaks of the very event that Peter refers to here; the unveiling, or return of Christ.

The evangel ^(1:10)

Concerning which salvation the prophets seek out and search out, who prophesy concerning the grace which is for you ... To whom it was revealed that, not to themselves, but to you they dispensed them, of which you were now informed through those who are bringing the evangel to you by holy spirit dispatched from heaven ...

> Believing Israel could look back to the prophets who searched out their destiny, and those bringing the evangel (gospel) to them now inform them, or remind them, of their expectation. How different this is from Paul's evangel which talked of SECRETS that were *unsearchable*.

Peter's evangel and Paul's evangel are not the same!

> Peter's evangel, spoken to believing Israel, was not a *secret*. It was simply that which the prophets had foretold. Israel would one day be restored, renewed and regenerated. Their Messiah (Christ) would return and reign. Paul's evangel, spoken to the Body of Christ, was a secret that was only revealed through him when God determined the time was right. His evangel spoke of the *Body of Christ*, a *new creation* (not just a regeneration), with no barrier between Jew and Gentile.

How then should you live? (1:13)

Be *sober* as you expect the grace that will be brought at the unveiling of Jesus Christ.

> We see this unveiling of Jesus Christ in the book of Revelation, which opens with the words, *The unveiling of Jesus Christ.* (Revelation 1:1)

As obedient children, not configuring to the former desires, in your ignorance, but, according as He Who calls you is holy, you also BECOME HOLY IN ALL BEHAVIOR, *because it is written that, Holy shall you be, for I am holy.*

> This is a direct reference from Leviticus 11:44; 19:2 and 20:7.

The Father ... is judging impartially ACCORDING TO EACH ONE'S WORK ... *Behave, for the time of your sojourn, with fear ...*

> Believing Israel is being judged based upon works, whereas Paul's evangel informs the Body of Christ that they are judged strictly by faith apart from works. (Romans 4:1-3)

> As for believing Israel; why is holy behavior important? They were not ransomed from their vain behavior with corruptible things like silver or gold, *but with the precious blood of Christ, as of a flawless and unspotted lamb.* (1:19)

Love one another (1:22)

Love one another out of a true heart earnestly, having been regenerated, not of corruptible seed but of incorruptible, through the word of God, living and permanent ... Now this is the declaration which is being brought to you in the evangel.

CHAPTER 2

Become mature (2:1)

Put off malice, guile, hypocrisies, envies and all vilifications. *Long for the unadulterated milk of the word that by it you may be growing into salvation.*

A holy priesthood (2:4)

As the Lord was rejected by men yet chosen by God and held in honor, *you also as living stones are being built up a spiritual house, into a holy priesthood, to offer up spiritual sacrifices, most acceptable to God through Jesus Christ.*

Priesthood = ISRAEL

Remember Paul's word to the Body of Christ. There is one mediator – Christ. (1 Timothy 2:5) There is no room for a priesthood in Paul's words. All are parts of the Body. All are Christ's ambassadors, not priests. (2 Corinthians 5:18-21) Clearly Peter speaks to a different audience, with words that resonate with believing Israel. They are priests, and they will serve as God's mediators to humanity in the final eons upon the earth after Christ's return.

It is *believing* Israel that has the honor, for the unbelieving are as a stone rejected by the builder; stumbling and stubborn. (2:7) *Yet you are a chosen race, a "royal priesthood," a "holy nation."* (2:9) This clearly fits Israel, for what other nation could be referred to as a *holy nation*?

The purpose of the holy priesthood (2:9)

... so that you should be recounting the virtues of Him Who calls you out of darkness into His marvelous light, who once were "not a people" yet now are the people of God, who "have not enjoyed mercy," yet now are "being showed mercy."

This is a direct reference to Hosea 1:9-11 which clearly speaks of Israel, and not of the nations.

The purpose of the priesthood is to display to humanity God's virtues, and this will surely take place in the final eons upon the earth when believing Israel will serve as God's priesthood. Once exiled and scattered and not a nation nor a people, once again upon being restored will Israel be a nation and a people for the purpose of recounting God's virtues to humanity.

Ideal behavior among those of the nations (2:11)

As sojourners and expatriates, abstain from fleshly lusts that war against the soul, and exhibit *ideal behavior* among the nations. So as the nations speak poorly of you, your ideal acts will cause them to glorify God *in the day of visitation.* (i.e. when Christ returns)

So the reason ideal acts are important is that they will have the effect of causing the nations to understand their error when Christ returns, even though they might speak poorly of Israel in the present day (when Peter wrote).

Be Subjected (2:13)

Be subject to every human creation because of the Lord; kings, governors, those sent for vengeance upon evildoers. By doing good you will be muzzling the ignorance of imprudent men. *Honor all; love the brotherhood; fear God; honor the king.*

Domestics should be subject to their owners, not only if their owner is good and lenient, but even if he may be crooked. *For what credit is it if, sinning and being buffeted, you will be enduring it? But if, doing good and suffering, you will be enduring, this is grace with God.*

Christ's example (2:21)

Christ suffered for your sakes, leaving you a *copy*, that you should be following up in His footprints. He did not sin, when He was reviled He did not revile, and when He suffered He did not threaten; *yet gave it over to Him Who is judging justly.*

He *carries up our sins in His body on to the pole* (**cross**), *that, coming away from sins,* WE SHOULD BE LIVING FOR RIGHTEOUSNESS; *by Whose welt you were healed. For you were as straying sheep, but now you* TURNED BACK *to the Shepherd and Supervisor of your souls.*

CHAPTER 3

Husbands and wives (3:1)

Wives are to be subject to their husbands; *that if any are stubborn also, as to the word, they will be gained without a word through the behavior of their wives, being spectators of your pure behavior ...*

Those who are *spectators* and who observe the willful subjection of wives will be influenced, even if they may be stubborn as to the *spoken* word.

And let it not be a woman's outward adornment that is observed; the braiding of hair, gold adornments or their clothing; but that which is hidden in the heart, such as a meek and quiet spirit.

There were examples of old that subjected themselves and had a meek and quiet spirit, such as Sarah who obeyed Abraham. Peter is not providing a timeless and specific list of things for women to wear or not wear (e.g. gold adornments). His point is simply that women were to exhibit meekness and a quiet spirit, thereby setting them apart from those of the nations in that day.

Holiness simply means set apart, distinguished, or different. (Although in our present day holiness seems to be more associated with specific lists of do's and don'ts created by man.)

Husbands are to give honor to the female as to a weaker vessel.

Proper behavior for all (3:8)

All are to be:

- ✓ Sympathetic
- ✓ Fond of the brethren
- ✓ Tenderly compassionate
- ✓ Of a humble disposition
- ✓ Not rendering evil for evil
- ✓ Not reviling those who revile
- ✓ Be a blessing, as you enjoy blessing
- ✓ If you suffer because of righteousness, be happy.

Always be ready to tell of your expectation (3:15)

[Be] *ever ready with a defense for everyone who is demanding from you an account concerning the expectation in you, but with meekness and fear, having a good conscience, that, in what they are speaking against you as of evildoers, they may be mortified, who traduce your good behavior in Christ.*

The context is suffering. If those who are in the midst of suffering can give an account of their expectation, what a powerful impact this will have on those who speak and do evil. The example of Christ is then given ...

For Christ died for man's sins though He was just, so that He may be leading men to God. He was put to death in flesh, but vivified in spirit.

The spirits in jail (3:19)

Christ, vivified in spirit, went *to the spirits in jail ... and He heralds to those once stubborn, when the patience of God awaited in the days of Noah ...*

This is an interesting side-note. Clearly these *spirits* are not human souls, for those who died in the days of Noah still sleep, awaiting the resurrection. And clearly this takes place not while Christ was entombed for three days as some speculate, but after He was *vivified* (made alive). These spirits are clearly *messengers* (angels) who are *jailed.* More information about this is provided in 2 Peter 2:4 where we learn that these are *sinning messengers* who are in *the gloomy caverns of Tartarus ... kept for chastening judging.*

Baptism is saving you (3:21)

The eight souls saved on the ark built by Noah are used as a *representation* of baptism which *is now saving you also (not the putting off of the filth of the flesh, but the inquiry of a good conscience to God), through the resurrection of Jesus Christ.*

> This does not refer to a baptism that cleanses the flesh, but *the inquiry of a good conscience to God.* Clearly it is not the physical water that is important, but the inner effects. Let us also keep in mind that while water baptism was always a part of the evangel proclaimed to the Circumcision (believing Israel) which is Peter's audience here, it did not accompany Paul's evangel to the Body of Christ. The *one baptism* of Ephesians 4:5 is clearly spiritual baptism. But to believing Israel, baptism and repentance were always essentials for entrance into the kingdom to be restored upon the earth. (Acts 2:38)

Christ in heaven (3:22)

... through the resurrection of Jesus Christ, Who is at God's right hand, being gone into heaven, messengers and authorities and power being subjected to Him.

> Christ is presently in heaven. Some claim He has returned in some sense already, but if this were true it would have occurred sometime following the death of the apostles, for Peter here tells us He is in heaven and there is no other apostolic writing that tells us otherwise, other than Revelation which has not yet taken place.
>
> Christ will return for the Body of Christ, calling us heavenward (1 Thessalonians 4:13ff) and He will subsequently return to the earth where He will reign, with believing Israel serving as His priesthood. But presently He is in the heavens. It is also interesting to consider He is *at God's right hand* (3:22). If the Trinitarian position were true, following the resurrection and glorification of Christ would He not occupy His place in the heavens as God. Instead there is still a distinction; God the Father, and at His right hand Jesus Christ His Son.

CHAPTER 4

God's will; not human desires (4:1)

Christ suffered in flesh *for our sakes*. Arm yourselves with the same thought. The one suffering in flesh *has ceased his sins*; not spending his lifetime in flesh in human desires, but God's will. As one suffers he is not living in his own desires but is focused on God.

Distinct from the nations [(4:3)]

The nations display their intentions: Wantonness, lusts, debauches, revelries, drinking bouts, illicit idolatries. They think it strange you do not do the same, and they calumniate [blaspheme] you.

> Some have the notion that "blaspheme" means to claim one is God. The Pharisees accused Jesus of blaspheme when He claimed to be the Son of God, or when He claimed the authority to forgive sins. But the Greek "blasphemos" simply means to speak "harmfully." When used of God the translation is blaspheme. When used of man the same Greek word is translated calumniate.

Judging the living and the dead [(4:5)]

[He is ready] *to judge the living and the dead. For for this an evangel is brought to the dead also, that they may be judged, indeed, according to men in flesh, yet should be living according to God, in spirit.*

> It is not that an evangel is proclaimed to those who are dead, for Scripture tells us that the dead know nothing. They are not in a conscious state and could not, therefore, hear. The point being made here is that those who are dead *had* heard an evangel while they were living, so that they could be judged on the day of judgment, in accordance with their acts while in the flesh. In all eras God desires man to live in accord with His spirit, and not in accord with the will of the flesh.

The end is near ... how to live [(4:7)]

The believer should be sane, sober for prayers, and have love. *Love is covering a multitude of sins.* Believers are to be hospitable to one another without murmuring.

> At the time he wrote, Peter clearly believed the end was near.

Use the grace given [(4:10)]

Each, as he has received a gracious gift, should use it *as ideal administrators of the varied grace of God.*

> The notion here is that God gives different kinds of grace to each individual, and whatever the gift it should be used among the ecclesia.

Speaking, as the oracles of God. *Dispensing,* out of the strength God furnishes. And the purpose is that in all God may be glorified.

Trials and suffering (4:12)

As you participate in the sufferings of Christ, rejoice; exalting in the unveiling of His glory. If reproached in the name of Christ, be happy, *for the spirit of glory and power, and that of God, has come to rest in you.*

But this is not so if one suffers for doing evil; for being a murderer, or thief, or interfering in others' affairs. Glorify God in being a Christian. Let those suffering according to God's will commit their souls to a faithful Creator in doing good.

The judgment is to begin from the house of God ...

> Surely this will be the case in the days of Revelation, when Israel will face severe trials as the day of Judgment arrives.

CHAPTER 5

Elders ... shepherd the flocklet (5:1)

Peter identifies himself as a *fellow elder* and *a participant of the glory about to be revealed.*

> Again we see that Peter believed the end was near.

The elders are to *shepherd the flocklet of God,* and:

- ✓ Supervise not out of compulsion, but voluntarily and eagerly.
- ✓ Become models for the flocklet; don't lord it over them.
- ✓ *When the Chief Shepherd is manifested, you shall be requited* (paid) *with an unfading wreath of glory.*

> Note the similarity to Peter's own commission in John 21:15-19, when the Lord commanded him to *"Shepherd My sheep."*

Younger men ... subjection and humility (5:5)

Be subject to the elder ... [Wear] humility with one another, for God is resisting the proud, yet is giving grace to the humble. Be humbled ... under God, that He should be exalting you in season, tossing your entire worry on Him, for He is caring concerning you.

> An *elder* does not appear to be a "position" within the ecclesia, but is contrasted with "younger men" and would seem to imply maturity.

Final instructions (5:8)

Be sober. Watch! For ... the Adversary is walking about as a roaring lion, seeking someone to swallow up. Withstand the Adversary, solid in the faith.

A word to those suffering ^(5:10)

While suffering briefly, the God of all grace calls you into His eonian glory in Christ. *He will be adjusting, establishing, firming, founding you.*

Signature ^(5:12)

Peter writes *through Silvanus*. He sends greetings from Mark, and from the ecclesia in Babylon.

SUMMARY

From this letter we can develop a picture of the situation the believers faced. They faced trials and testing; but this would result in applause, glory and honor at the unveiling of Jesus Christ. And what was their expectation at this unveiling of Jesus Christ? Thru Christ's resurrection they have a *living expectation* for the enjoyment of an *allotment incorruptible,* being preserved for them until it is *revealed in the last era.*

As they awaited Christ's return, Peter calls them to be sober; obedient and not conforming to their former desires when they were ignorant of their expectation. They were to be holy in all behavior.

Peter exhorts them: Love one another. Become mature and put off malice, guile, hypocrisy and envy. For there were *living stones* being built into a spiritual house and a *holy priesthood.* And as such they should abstain from fleshly lusts and exhibit *ideal behavior* among the nations, thereby causing the nations to glorify God *in the day of visitation.*

Be subject to every human creature. Do good and endure suffering. Be living for righteousness.

All should exhibit proper behavior; sympathy, love for the brethren, compassion, humility, not rendering evil for evil. They were to be a blessing, and always ready to tell of their expectation with meekness.

Seek God's will, not human desires. The nations display wantonness, lust, debauchery, revelry, drinking bouts, illicit idolatries; but they were not to do the same.

The end is near. Be sane, sober for prayers, and have love. Be hospitable to one another without murmuring. As each has been given a gracious gift, use it as an ideal administrator.

Rejoice in suffering. Exult in the unveiling of His glory. Be happy if reproached in the name of Christ.

Elders are to shepherd. Young men are to be subject to the elders with humility. Watch! Withstand the Adversary who walks about as a lion seeking someone to swallow up. Be solid in the faith.

2 Peter

An Overview of the Scriptures, by
BOB EVELY © *2018.*
An Independent Minister of Christ Jesus,
Of the church at Wilmore, Kentucky

Circumcision	Uncircumcision	
James		45 AD
Jude		46 AD
	1 Thessalonians	50-52 AD
	2 Thessalonians	52-53 AD
Hebrews		53-54 AD
	Galatians (early theory)	54 AD
1/2/3 John		55-56 AD
	1 Corinthians	Spring 57 AD
	2 Corinthians	Fall 57 AD
	Galatians	Winter 57 AD
	Romans	Spring 58 AD
1 Peter		60 AD
2 Peter		**61 AD**
	Colossians	61-62 AD
	Ephesians	61-62 AD
	Philemon	62-63 AD
	Philippians	63 AD
	1 Timothy	67 AD
	Titus	67 AD
	2 Timothy	Spring 68 AD

We now turn to a second letter written by Peter.

WARNING!

We must keep in mind that Peter was entrusted with the evangel of the Circumcision. This letter is directed to the believing "sheep of Israel" within the early ecclesia, and not to the Body of Christ. All Scripture is for our benefit, but not all Scripture is written directly TO us in this present age. We must take great care not to force direct application of this writing into our present context. God clearly deals differently with different people groups (Israel versus the nations) and in different eras.

CHAPTER 1

The address on the envelope (1:1)

From Peter ...

To those chancing upon an equally precious faith with us.

> While ambiguous as to his audience (those chancing upon an equally precious faith with us), Peter is always associated with the believers of Israel.

Participants of the divine nature (1:3)

Christ's divine power tends toward life and devoutness. Thru the recognition of Him, we have been given the precious and greatest promises, that you may become participants of the divine nature, fleeing from the corruption in the world by lust.

> Remember that "we" and "us" refer to those Peter associates himself with and those to whom this letter is written; the believers among ISRAEL.

Exhibit ideal behavior (1:5)

Employ diligence in your faith, supplying virtue, knowledge, self-control, endurance, devoutness, brotherly fondness, love. Increase in these and be not idle nor unfruitful in the recognition of our Lord, Jesus Christ. Any for whom these are not present are blind, having closed their eyes, and they are oblivious to the cleansing from the penalties of their sins of old. Thru ideal acts confirm your calling and choice, and you will not be tripping. And it will be richly supplied to you entrance into the *eonian kingdom*.

> Remember, the expectation of believing Israel is entrance into the kingdom to be established by Christ upon the earth. Those "tripping" and not enduring will be prevented from entering this *eonian kingdom* in the eons to come following Christ's return. For Israel believing thru the Circumcision evangel, faith plus works are required.

Reminders so they will remember after Peter's death (1:12)

I shall ever be reminding you about these things, even though you are aware of and have been established in the present truth. For as long as I am in this tabernacle I will rouse you with a reminder. I am aware that my tabernacle will be put off swiftly as our Lord made evident to me. But I will endeavor to have you, after my exodus, to make mention of these things.

Peter knows the end of his life is approaching. And while these are truths the believers among Israel have already heard, Peter sees need to REMIND them so they will remember after his death.

An eye-witness of the Lord's glory (1:16)

We make known to you the power and presence of our Lord Jesus Christ not by following myths, but by being spectators of His magnificence. For He received from God the Father the honor and glory of the voice, *This is My Son, the Beloved, in Whom I delight.* And this voice we hear from out of heaven, being together with Him in the holy mountain. And we are having the prophetic word more confirmed, which you, doing ideally, are heeding.

This is in reference to the time when Peter, James and John witnessed the transfiguration of Christ, and Peter here reports the words they all heard coming from out of heaven. (Matthew 17:1-8) Peter was a spectator; an eye-witness of God's glorification of Christ.

The nature of prophecy (1:21)

Not by the will of man was prophecy carried on at any time, but, being carried on by holy spirit, holy men of God speak.

Not only does this tell us the nature of prophecy in general, but from the context we learn that Peter's own words are prophecy; a word from God. Prophecy is not men speaking of their own will, but they speak as they are "carried on" by the holy spirit.

CHAPTER 2

Beware of false teachers (2:1)

There came to be among the people false prophets, as among you there will be false teachers; who will smuggle in destructive sects, disowning the Owner Who buys them; bringing swift destruction upon themselves. Many will follow out of their wantonness, because of whom the glory of the truth will be calumniated. In greed and with suave words they will traffic in you.

If God did not spare sinning messengers but thrust them into the gloomy caverns of *Tartarus*, keeping them for *chastening judging;* and if God did not spare the ancient world but brought a deluge on the world of the irreverent, sparing only Noah; and if God condemned Sodom and Gomorrah, reducing them to cinders as an example for those about to be irreverent, rescuing only Lot; the Lord knows how to rescue the devout out of trial while keeping the unjust for chastening in the day of judging, especially those going after the flesh in defiling lust and despising lordship.

Tartarus, one of three Greek words often translated hell, is a place reserved not for humans, but for the *chastening judging* of messengers/angels. *Chastening judging* is not eternal torment as many Bible translations lead us to believe. Chastening carries the notion of corrective discipline with the intent of bringing reform.

We note that despising lordship or a refusal to become subject to God, is an offense deserving chastening judging.

Characteristics of the unjust [(2:11)]
- ✓ Lust of the flesh that defiles
- ✓ They despise lordship (being subjected)
- ✓ Self-gratification
- ✓ They calumniate things of glory without trembling
- ✓ They calumniate that in which they are ignorant in their corruption
- ✓ They shall be requited with the wages of injustice
- ✓ They luxuriate in love feasts
- ✓ They have the distended eyes of an adulteress
- ✓ They do not stop from sin
- ✓ They lure unstable souls
- ✓ They have a heart exercised by greed
- ✓ They left the straight path and were led astray
- ✓ They follow the path of Balaam of Beor
- ✓ They lure by the lusts of the flesh
- ✓ They promise freedom, but are slaves of corruption

A warning to backsliders [(2:20)]
If while fleeing from the defilements of the world by recognizing our Lord and Savior, they become again involved in these things, their last state is worse than the first.

CHAPTER 3

This letter is a reminder [(3:1)]
This is my second epistle, to arouse your sincere comprehension by a reminder of what the holy prophets said, and of the precepts of your apostles.

Whereas Paul introduced SECRETS; new information previously concealed; Peter notes that he is simply providing REMINDERS of what the prophets had previously said.

Scoffers will come in the last days ... (3:3)

... going in accord with their own desires, saying, "Where is the promise of His presence? All is continuing as it was since the beginning of creation."

They forgot that the then-world perished (3:5)

There were heavens of old, an earth cohering out of water and through water by the word of God, through which the then-world being deluged by water, perished.

> At first we might think this refers back to the flood in Noah's day, but an earth *cohering out of water and through water* seems more like the description of the earth in its state of void and chaos, before the creation described in Genesis 1.
>
> *And Elohim said: Let an atmosphere come to be in the midst of the waters, that it may be separating waters from waters. And it came to be so. Elohim made the atmosphere and separated the waters under the atmosphere from the waters above the atmosphere ... And Elohim said: Let the waters under the heavens flow together into one confluence, that the dry ground may appear. And it came to be so. And Elohim called the dry ground land, and the confluence of the waters he called seas.* (Genesis 1:6-10)
>
> There was a "then world" that once existed until, for unrevealed reasons, the earth BECAME chaos; (Genesis 1:2) after which the creation (or re-creation) took place as described in Genesis. We will consider this in greater depth when considering Genesis.

Judgment is coming (3:7)

The heavens now, and the earth, by the same word, are stored with fire, being kept for the day of judging and destruction of irreverent men.

In God's timing (3:8)

One day is with the Lord as a thousand years. The Lord is not tardy as to the promise as some are deeming tardiness.

> The scoffers reasoned that since God had delayed for so long, judgment was not coming at all. Peter points out that God works within His timeframe, not man's.

Why does God delay? (3:9)

He is patient; not intending any to perish, but all to make room for repentance.

The Day of the Lord ... (3:10)

... will arrive as a thief. The heavens will pass with a booming noise. The elements will be dissolved by combustion; the earth and the works in it.

> Peter speaks of the passing of the present earth, making way for the new heaven and new earth. *And I perceived a new heaven and a new earth, for the former heaven and the former earth pass away, and the sea is no more.* (Revelation 21:1)

So how should we live? (3:11)

With holy behavior and devoutness.

God's Day: New heavens and earth (3:12)

Hoping for and hurrying the presence of God's day, because of which the heavens will be dissolved and the elements decompose by combustion. According to His promises we are hoping for new heavens and a new earth, in which righteousness is dwelling.

> The Bible makes reference to three "days." Man's day is the day in which we live, where man appears to reign. The Lord's day, or the Day of the Lord, is the day when the Lord returns to reign. God's day begins with the introduction of the new heavens and earth as we see noted here and in Revelation 21:1.

How then should we live? (3:14)

Endeavor to be found by Him in peace, unspotted and flawless. Be deeming the patience of the Lord's salvation.

> Here salvation clearly refers to the day when the Lord will return to rescue the patient and enduring believers who are experiencing hardship. These words were a comfort to those suffering hardship in Peter's day, and they will be welcome words in the days leading up to the return of the Lord; commonly referred to as the Great Tribulation.

As Paul also writes to you ... (3:15)

... in which some things are hard to apprehend. The unlearned and unstable are twisting.

> We remember that Paul was commissioned to go to those of Israel and *also* those of the nations. (Acts 9:15) In Acts we see him beginning in the synagogues, and when he is expelled he then goes to those of the nations. Paul's epistles are addressed primarily to those within the Body of Christ, or the ecclesia comprised of Jews and Gentiles with no distinction or preference.

> But somewhere along the way Paul directed a letter to those of Israel, as Peter mentions here. Some speculate that Hebrews was written by Paul, although its author is not revealed in the letter. Whether Paul wrote Hebrews or not, it is clear from Peter's comments here that Paul did address the believers among Israel at some point.
>
> Also note the words, *as the rest of the scriptures also.* (v. 16) Paul's writings are here spoken of by Peter as *scriptures.*

Beware of deception ^(3:17)

Be on guard lest you are led away with deception. Grow in grace, and in the knowledge of our Lord and Saviour Jesus Christ. To Him be glory, now; and for *the day of the eon.* (3:18)

> An eon is a period of time with a beginning and an end, though it is often translated eternal or endless in many versions. *The day of the eon* in this passage makes reference to an eon other than the present one; presumably the eon when the Lord returns since that is the present context.

SUMMARY

From this letter we can develop a picture of the situation the believers faced. This was a time of great persecution at the hand of Nero. Peter tells them as long as he was in *this tabernacle* he would rouse them with a *reminder* of these things.

They were to flee from the corruption of the world by lust, thru Christ's divine power that enables them to become participants of the divine nature.

There were to exhibit ideal behavior; virtue, knowledge, self-control, endurance, devoutness, brotherly fondness, and love. They were to confirm their calling and choice thru ideal acts; and they will be richly supplied with entrance into the *eonian kingdom.*

They were to beware of false teachers, and the characteristics of the unjust: Lust of the flesh, self-gratification, rejection of lordship, calumniating things of glory, luxuriating in love feasts, having the eyes of an adulteress, and greed. These ones lure away unstable souls. They were to beware of backsliding, as their last state would be worse than the first.

Peter warned the scoffers would come, saying: "Where is this promised presence? All continues as it has since the beginning of creation." But to the

Lord a day is as a thousand years. He is not tardy. He is patient, not intending any to perish, making room for repentance. The Day of the Lord will come as a thief. Therefore they were to have holy behavior and devoutness as they hoped for a new heavens and a new earth in which the righteousness would dwell. They were to endeavor to be found by Him in peace; unspotted and flawless. Beware of deception!

1,2,3 John

An Overview of the Scriptures, by
BOB EVELY © 2018.
An Independent Minister of Christ Jesus,
Of the church at Wilmore, Kentucky

Circumcision	Uncircumcision	
James		45 AD
Jude		46 AD
	1 Thessalonians	50-52 AD
	2 Thessalonians	52-53 AD
Hebrews		53-54 AD
	Galatians (early theory)	54 AD
1/2/3 John		**55-56 AD**
	1 Corinthians	Spring 57 AD
	2 Corinthians	Fall 57 AD
	Galatians	Winter 57 AD
	Romans	Spring 58 AD
1 Peter		60 AD
2 Peter		61 AD
	Colossians	61-62 AD
	Ephesians	61-62 AD
	Philemon	62-63 AD
	Philippians	63 AD
	1 Timothy	67 AD
	Titus	67 AD
	2 Timothy	Spring 68 AD

There is no address on John's first letter. The second is addressed, *From the Elder; to the chosen lady and her children whom I am loving in truth.* This is a bit cryptic. Was John using a code, due to the persecution the believers faced? Was he simply being poetic? We can only speculate on his reasons. But from the context and the many similarities in word and phrase structure with John's gospel, clearly the writer is the apostle John.

The third letter is addressed, *From the Elder; to Gaius, the beloved.* But again, we see many similarities to John's gospel; light vs. darkness, the

Word, the Light. And reference is made to the transfiguration of Christ, to which only the apostles Peter, James and John were witnesses.

In every recorded instance, John's ministry is limited to the Circumcision (Israel). He views the nations as being outside of his scope. (3 John 5-8) He makes a distinction between *ours* (Israel) and the whole world. (1 John 2:2) He places great emphasis on his personal connection with Jesus during His earthly ministry. (1 John 1:1-4) At the Jerusalem conference, James, Cephas (Peter) and John represent the Circumcision, and Paul the Uncircumcision. (Galatians 2:6-9) In that instance John, along with James and Peter, are referred to as *pillars* within the ecclesia of Jewish believers.

We remember that during Christ's kingdom ministry the nations are blessed only thru Israel. We see this expressed in John's gospel and letters; in God's love for the world. (John 3:16)

WARNING!

We must correctly cut, or rightly divide, the word of truth. (2 Timothy 2:15)

John's letters are directed to the believing "sheep of Israel" within the early ecclesia, and not to the Body of Christ. All Scripture is for our benefit, but not all Scripture is written directly TO us in this present age. We must take great care not to force direct application of this writing into our present context. God clearly deals differently with different people groups (Israel versus the nations) and in different eras.

Now let's consider what John has to say.

CHAPTER 1

An eyewitness account concerning LIFE (1:1)

That which was from the beginning which we have heard and seen. The life was manifested. We are testifying and reporting to you the *life eonian* which was toward the Father and was manifested to us.

> *That which we have heard and seen* is concerned with the word of life. *Life eonian* refers to having life in the coming age/eon when the kingdom is established upon the earth with Christ's return. Those not having life eonian will not enjoy life in that coming age, although this will not prevent them from

the ultimate reconciliation of all at the end of the ages. (1 Corinthians 15:21-28)

The purpose of this account (1:3)

That you too may be having fellowship with us, and with the Father and with His Son. These things we write that our joy may be full.

The message we heard from Him ... LIGHT (1:5)

God is light, and darkness in Him there is none. If we say we are fellowshipping with Him and are walking in darkness, we are lying. If we are walking in light as He is in the light, we fellowship with one another and His blood is cleansing us from every sin.

Acknowledge your sins (1:8)

If we say we have no sin we are deceiving ourselves. If we avow our sins He is faithful and just; pardoning our sins and cleansing us from all injustice. If we say we have not sinned, we are making Him a liar and His word is not in us.

CHAPTER 2

Be not sinning (2:1)

I write that you may not be sinning. If anyone is sinning we have an entreater with the Father; Jesus Christ, the just. He is the *propitiatory shelter* concerned with our sins; yet not ours only but with the whole world. If we know Him we keep His precepts. If one says he knows Him but is not keeping His precepts he is a liar. If one keeps His word, in this one the love of God is perfected. If one remains in Him, he will walk as He walks.

The true light is appearing (2:8)

The darkness is passing and the true light is already appearing.

As John writes there is a sense that the kingdom to come upon the earth is very near. God's plan to temporarily set aside Israel for an extended period of time, and a pause in the events leading to Christ's return, is not seen by John.

Love your brother (2:9)

If one says he is in the light but hates his brother, he is a liar and is in darkness, and the darkness blinds him so he is not aware where he is going. He who loves his brother is in the light.

We see much repetition in this letter. Perhaps repetition is needed by the stubborn and stiff-necked people to whom John writes.

Why am I writing to you? (2:12)

Your sins have been forgiven you thru His name,
You know Him Who is from the beginning,
You have conquered the wicked one,
You know the Father,
You are strong and the word of God is remaining in you,

Love not the world (2:15)

... neither that which is in the world. If one loves the world, the love of the Father is not in him. Everything in the world; desire of the flesh, desire of the eyes, the ostentation of living; is not of the Father. The world is passing by, yet he who is doing the will of God is *remaining for the eon.*

> *Remaining for the eon* refers to life in the age/eon to come when Christ returns. Some will not enjoy life in that eon, though this will not exclude them from the reconciliation of all at the end of the eons.

Many antichrists ... it is the last hour (2:18)

As you hear the antichrist is coming, now also there have come to be many antichrists; whence we know it is the last hour. Out of us they come, but they were not of us, else they would have remained with us. You have an anointing from the Holy One.

> These antichrists are those within the ecclesia that had turned against Christ (hence anti-Christs). Here we see reference to many antichrists acting in the spirit of THE Antichrist of whom we read in Revelation.
>
> And with these many antichrists that had been WITHIN the ecclesia and that were now turning against the ecclesia, we see the growing apostasy. The ecclesia was not growing stronger; it was weakening with many turning away.

I write because you are acquainted with the truth (2:21)

He who denies, saying "Jesus is not the Christ" is the antichrist. He who disowns the Son has not the Father. He who avows the Son has the Father also.

The promise for those "remaining" in the Son (2:24)

... *the life eonian.*

> Some were turning against Christ, and they will forfeit life in the eon to come when Christ returns, though this will not be their final condition.

No need for teachers [(2:26)]

The anointing you received from Him remains in you, and you have no need that anyone may be teaching you. His anointing is teaching you concerning all.

> As apostasy grew within the ecclesia some teachers were apparently responsible for the turning away. John's audience is encouraged not to trust teachers (for they might be misled), but to be led by the holy spirit.

> And again we point out that the ecclesia was not growing stronger, but was weakening with this apostasy; to the point where the flock could no longer trust teachers and needed to rely directly on the holy spirit for truth.

Remain in Him ... [(2:28)]

... that if He should be manifested, we can have boldness and not be put to shame in His presence. Everyone doing righteousness is begotten of Him.

CHAPTER 3

Children of God compared with the world [(3:1)]

We are called children of God because of the love the Father has given us. Therefore the world does not know us, for it did not know Him. We are now children of God, and when He is manifested we will be like Him.

> John suggests a change will take place when Christ is manifested (when He returns). When that happens, the believers among Israel will be like Him.

Remain in Him [(3:4)]

Everyone remaining in Him is not sinning. Everyone sinning sees Him not, and does not know Him.

> Unlike the "faith alone" that Paul speaks of, in the Circumcision evangel there is always the additional requirement of works. Yes, Paul encourages good works in response to God's grace, but the Circumcision writers (Peter, John, etc.) require works as a condition to entering the kingdom when it is established upon the earth.

He who is sinning is of the Adversary [(3:7)]

From the beginning the Adversary (Satan) is sinning. The Son of God was manifested to annul the acts of the Adversary. Everyone begotten of God is not doing sin. This is how it becomes apparent who are the children of God versus the children of the Adversary. Everyone not doing righteousness is not of God.

Even Peter, when he attempted to take matters into his own hands and unknowingly interrupt the plan God was unfolding, is referred to as Satan. For he was acting as an *adversary* to God's plan. Jesus said to Peter, "Get behind me *Satan.*"

Love thy brother, not just in word but in acts (3:10)

Everyone not loving his brother is not of God. Love one another; not like Cain who was of the wicked one and slayed his brother. He slayed him because his acts were wicked, and his brother's acts were just.

Don't marvel if the world hates you. We have proceeded out of death into life, for we are loving our brethren. He who is not loving his brethren is a man-killer, and has no *life eonian*.

He, for our sakes, laid down His soul. By this we know love. We ought to lay down our souls for the sake of the brethren.

If we have a livelihood in this world and behold a brother having need, how is the love of God remaining in him if he locks his compassions? We should not be loving in word, but in acts and truth.

Boldness toward God if our heart does not censure us (3:19)

If our heart is not censuring us, we have boldness toward God, and whatsoever we may be requesting we are obtaining from Him, for we are keeping His precepts and are doing what is pleasing in His sight.

Note the similarity to "Ask anything and it will be given to you." This is God's method during the kingdom age; with preparations being made for Christ's return and for the kingdom to be established upon the earth. But how different this is from God's method in the age Paul introduced, where grace is sufficient.

This is His precept (3:23)

Be believing in the name of His Son, Jesus Christ. Be loving one another. The one keeping His precepts is remaining in Him, and He in him. This is how we know He is remaining in us; by the spirit He gives us.

CHAPTER 4

Test the spirits (4:1)

Do not believe every spirit, but test the spirits to see if they are of God. Many false prophets have come. Every spirit avowing Jesus Christ having come in flesh is of God. Every spirit not avowing Jesus the Lord having come in the flesh is not of God; it is that of the antichrist you heard is coming who is now already in the world. Greater is He within you than he who is within the world. They are of the world, and the world hears them. We are of God. He who knows God, hears us. This is how we know the spirit of truth vs. the spirit of deception.

> The anti-christs were, then, those teaching that Christ was not "of God."

Love one another (4:7)

Be loving one another, for love is of God. Everyone who is loving God is begotten of God and knows God. God is love. The love of God was manifested when He dispatched His only begotten Son into the world that we should be living thru Him. He is a *propitiatory shelter* concerned with our sins. If God loves us thus, we ought to love one another.

No one has ever gazed upon God. If we love one another, God is remaining in us and His love is perfected in us. And this is how we know; He gave us His spirit. The Father dispatched the Son, the Saviour of the world.

Whoever avows that Jesus is the Son of God, God is remaining in him and he in God. He who is remaining in love is remaining in God, and God is remaining in him. In this is love perfected with us, that we may have boldness in the day of judging. Fear is not in love. Perfect love casts out fear, for fear has chastening. He who is fearing is not perfected in love.

> The false teachers were opposing truth, claiming that Jesus was *not* the Son of God.

We love God for He first loves us. He who is not loving his brother whom he sees cannot be loving God Whom he has not seen.

CHAPTER 5

Love (continued) (5:1)

Everyone believing that Jesus is the Christ is begotten of God. Everyone who loves Him who begets (God) is also loving him also who is begotten. We know we are loving the children of God when we love God and do His precepts. This is the love of God; to keep His precepts. His precepts are not heavy. All that is begotten of God is conquering the world. Our faith is that which conquers the world.

The testimony that Jesus is the Son of God (5:6)

Jesus Christ is coming thru water and blood and spirit. These three testify. The testimony of God is greater than the testimony of men. He who believes in the Son of God has the testimony in himself. He who does not believe has not believed God or His testimony. This is the testimony; that God gives us *life eonian,* and this life is in His Son.

He who has the Son has the life. He who has not the Son of God has not the life.

These things I write to you, that you who believe in the name of the Son of God may see that you have life eonian. And if we should request anything according to His will, He is hearing us and we have that which is requested.

Requesting life for those sinning (5:16)

If one sees a brother sinning a sin not to death, and if he asks, He will give him life. All iniquity is sin, and there is a sin not to death.

Be not sinning (5:18)

Everyone begotten of God is not sinning. He is keeping himself, and the wicked one is not touching him. We are of God, and the whole world is lying in the wicked one.

The Son gives us comprehension of God (5:20)

The Son of God is arriving and has given us a comprehension; that we know the True One; the true God and life eonian.

Guard yourself from idols (5:21)

2 JOHN

The truth is remaining (:2)

The truth is remaining in us and will be with us for the eon. With us will be grace, mercy, and peace from God.

Love one another (:4)

I rejoiced that your children are walking in truth. Love one another. This is love; that we walk according to His precepts.

Deceivers (:7)

Many deceivers come out into the world, not avowing Jesus Christ coming in flesh. This is the deceiver and the antichrist. Don't destroy that for which you work. Be getting full wages.

> Again in John's second letter the apostasy within the ecclesia grows. There were MANY deceivers who were disputing the heart of truth; that Christ had come in the flesh.

Remain in the teaching (:9)

Those not remaining in the teaching of Christ has not God. Those remaining in the teaching have both the Father and the Son. If anyone comes not bringing this teaching, take them not into your home, and say not "Rejoice," else you participate in his wicked acts.

> Here we see the practice of "shunning" that is employed by the Amish, as well as other sects among Christianity.

I am coming to you (:12)

Having much to write to you, I resolved not to write, but am expecting to come to you and speak in person, that your joy may be full.

3 JOHN

Greatest joy ... to hear my children are walking in truth (:2)

I wish that you be prospering and sound, as your soul is prospering. I rejoiced when I heard the report that you are walking in the truth. I have no greater joy than to hear of *my children* walking in truth.

Working for the brethren ... walking worthily of God (:5)

You are being faithful when working for the brethren, and when strangers testify to your love in the sight of the ecclesia. You do ideal to send them forth worthily of God, for the sake of the Name, getting nothing from those of the nations. We ought to be fellow workers in the truth.

> Gaius is obviously a leader or teacher among the brethren, and is being instructed by John on providing leadership.

Problems with Diotrephes; foremost in the ecclesia (:9)

Diotrephes, fond of being foremost among the ecclesia, is not receiving us. If I come I will remind him of his acts; gossiping about us with wicked words and casting the brethren out of the ecclesia.

> This is perhaps the reason John wrote this letter. Diotrephes has allowed pride to take hold as he leads the ecclesia. He is fond of being foremost. He gossips about the apostle. He is casting brethren out of the ecclesia, clearly without good reason (else John would not find fault with him doing so).

A good word on behalf of Demetrius (:11)

He who is doing good is of God. He who is doing evil has not seen God. Demetrius has been attested by all and by the truth. We also are testifying.

It could be that Demetrius had been cast out of the ecclesia without good reason by Diotrephes.

I am planning to come (:13)

I had much to say, but do not want to write to you. I expect to see you immediately to speak in person.

SUMMARY

In John's letters we can clearly see the situation faced by the ecclesia comprised of Hebrew believers. There were false teachers, once a part of the ecclesia but who were now turning away from the truth and proclaiming that Christ did not really come in the flesh; that Jesus was not the Christ. The apostasy is clear even in John's final letter. So the ecclesia was not growing in number and becoming stronger; it was weakening due to this apostasy; this turning away. John even advised NOT to rely upon teachers within the ecclesia, but instead to seek truth directly from the holy spirit.

This growing apostasy is, I believe, the reason the Scriptures were "compiled" (the correct writings included) by the apostles themselves. How could they entrust the ecclesia of the next generation to "canonize" the Scriptures when already apostasy was rampant. How could they know that these false teachers would not play a part in the canonization process or in the preservation of truth. Peter also recognized this growing apostasy, and we will see that Paul did as well. It is my belief that Peter, Paul, and John played a part in preserving ("canonizing" if you will) the Scriptures for future generations. I highly recommend an excellent book that elaborates on this theory; *The Original Bible Restored* by Ernest Martin.

Now let us summarize the key points found in John's letters.

- ✓ Life eonian has been manifested.
- ✓ God is light; there is no darkness in Him.
- ✓ If we sin Christ is our Entreater with the Father, and our propitiatory shelter.
- ✓ Everything in the world; the desire of the flesh, the desire of the eyes, ostentation in living; is not of the Father.
- ✓ The antichrist is coming, and many antichrists have already come *out of us;* saying Jesus is not the Christ.
- ✓ You have no need of teachers; His anointing is teaching you.

✓ We are children of God, and the world does not know us.
✓ Perfect love casts out fear.

And how did John entreat his audience to live?

✓ *Walk* in the light.
✓ *Acknowledge* your sins, and He will pardon and cleanse us.
✓ Be not sinning.
✓ *Keep* His precepts.
✓ *Remain* in Him.
✓ *Walk* as He walks.
✓ *Love* your brother.
✓ Don't love the world or that which is in the world.
✓ *Do* the will of God.
✓ *Love* your brother not just in word but also in acts.
✓ *Do* what is pleasing in His sight.
✓ *Believe* in the name of His Son, Jesus Christ.
✓ *Love* one another.
✓ *Test* the spirits; many false prophets have come.
✓ *Love* God. God is love.
✓ *Avow* that Jesus is the Son of God.
✓ *Guard* yourself from idols.
✓ *Remain* in the teaching of Christ.
✓ *Walk* in truth.
✓ *Work* for the brethren.

John repeats many of these entreaties multiple times throughout his three epistles.

Jude

An Overview of the Scriptures, by
BOB EVELY © 2018.
An Independent Minister of Christ Jesus,
Of the church at Wilmore, Kentucky

Circumcision	Uncircumcision	
James		45 AD
Jude		46 AD
	1 Thessalonians	50-52 AD
	2 Thessalonians	52-53 AD
Hebrews		53-54 AD
	Galatians (early theory)	54 AD
1/2/3 John		55-56 AD
	1 Corinthians	Spring 57 AD
	2 Corinthians	Fall 57 AD
	Galatians	Winter 57 AD
	Romans	Spring 58 AD
1 Peter		60 AD
2 Peter		61 AD
	Colossians	61-62 AD
	Ephesians	61-62 AD
	Philemon	62-63 AD
	Philippians	63 AD
	1 Timothy	67 AD
	Titus	67 AD
	2 Timothy	Spring 68 AD

Jude (Judas) tells us he is a brother of James, and therefore the brother of Jesus. Remember that James was prominent among the Circumcision believers (Israel).

WARNING!

We must correctly cut, or rightly divide, the word of truth. (2 Timothy 2:15)

This letter is directed to the believing "sheep of Israel" within the early ecclesia, and not to the Body of Christ. All Scripture is for our benefit, but not all Scripture is written directly TO us in this present age. We must take great care not to force direct application of this writing into our present context. God clearly deals differently with different people groups (Israel versus the nations) and in different eras.

Now let's consider what Jude has to say.

CHAPTER 1

The address on the envelope (1:1)

From Judas;
To those called beloved, and kept by Jesus Christ.

Contend for the faith (:3)

I have found it necessary to write to you, *entreating you to contend for the faith.* Some irreverent men slip in, bartering God's grace for wantonness, and disowning our only Owner and Lord, Jesus Christ.

> Jude was writing to counter the false teachings that had infiltrated the ecclesia.

A reminder from Egypt (:5)

When the Lord saved the people out of Egypt He destroyed those who did not believe. And messengers who do not keep their own sovereignty but leave their own habitation He has kept in *imperceptible bonds under gloom for the judging of the great day.*

And Sodom and Gomorrah lie before us a specimen, experiencing the justice of *fire eonian.* These dreamers defile the flesh, repudiate lordship and calumniate glories.

> Consider from Genesis: The *sons of the elohim* take wives from the *daughters of the human.* (Genesis 6:2) Immediately thereafter we read that Yahweh Elohim declares: *His days will be 120 years.* The shortest span of life noted in Seth's line before this time is 753 years (not counting Enoch whose death is not recorded). This shortening of man's lifetime appears to be a direct response to the growing evil within man.
>
> It could be that *the sons of the elohim* may have been a particular line of men God had chosen to be His "To-Subjectors;" leaders among men chosen for the purpose of bringing other men into subjection to God. The practice of these

- 88 -

men marrying others outside of the line, thereby diluting the authority of the sons of the elohim, is what appears to be objectionable to God.

But it is possible that the elohim in this case are referring to celestial beings, commonly called *angels*, who have interacted with man. Jude v.6 refers to *messengers who keep not their own sovereignty, but leave their own habitation.* This could refer to angels intermarrying with humans, although the Jude reference does not tell us exactly how these beings have left "their own habitation." Since elohim can refer to celestial beings or humans, then, we cannot be definitive in our interpretation of this Genesis 6 passage. But it could tie-in with Jude v.6.

Woe to those who oppose (:11)

These calumniate what they are not acquainted with, as irrational animals. Woe to them. For they go in the way of Cain, Balaam and Korah; they perish. They come to your love feasts and carouse with you fearlessly. They are waterless clouds, unfruitful; frothing forth their own shame. The gloom of darkness has been kept for them for an eon.

They are murmurers, complainers, going according to their desires. Their mouth speaks pompous things.

Remember the declarations (:17)

Remember the declarations of the apostles who warned, *In the last time will be coming scoffers, going according to their own irreverent desires.* They have not the spirit.

Build yourselves up (:20)

Build yourselves up in your most holy faith. Pray in holy spirit. Keep yourself in the love of God. Anticipate the mercy of our Lord Jesus Christ for *life eonian.* Be merciful to those doubting. Others be saving; snatching them from the fire. Be merciful with fear, hating even the tunic spotted by the flesh.

SUMMARY

From this letter we can develop a picture of the situation the believers faced. Some had slipped in, misusing grace and introducing *wantonness;* disowning Christ. Jude entreats his audience to CONTEND FOR THE FAITH. He warns those that would oppose truth; they would perish as did Cain, Balaam and Korah in times past. There were those that were murmuring, complaining and following their own desires. But Jude reminds the faithful ones what the apostles had taught; that in the last time there would come scoffers going according to their own irreverent desires.

Jude entreats the ecclesia to:
- ✓ Build yourself up in faith.
- ✓ Pray.
- ✓ Keep yourselves in the love of God.
- ✓ Anticipate the mercy of our Lord Jesus Christ for life eonian.
- ✓ Be merciful to those who are doubting.

Jude is a prelude to Revelation. The central theme is the coming of the Lord in judgment on the irreverent. (v. 14-15)

𝕿𝖍𝖊 𝖂𝖆𝖎𝖙𝖎𝖓𝖌

Summary

An Overview of the Scriptures, by
BOB EVELY © *2018.*
An Independent Minister of Christ Jesus
Of the church at Wilmore, Kentucky

Throughout the four gospel accounts we see a distinctive Jewish focus. We find many Old Testament references. Jesus announces the restoration of the kingdom. But the king and the kingdom are rejected by the Jews who so anxiously awaited their coming, and the king is crucified.

Still, the evangel remains the same in the book of Acts when Peter (who was given the keys to the kingdom) proclaims the same message. Christ has been crucified and resurrected, but in the book of Acts it is still the kingdom to come upon the earth that is being proclaimed, and it is proclaimed exclusively to the Jews as was the case throughout Matthew. Salvation, or life in the eon to come, is life in the kingdom of the heavens when it comes upon the earth with Christ upon the throne.

The believers among Israel were awaiting the return of Christ. And as they awaited this event, the circumcision epistles addressed them; encouraging them to endure, even thru times of persecution. Remain true to the faith; and beware of false teachers that would mislead!

Throughout Acts we see the evangel of the kingdom continually rejected. When the kingdom is *finally* rejected at the end of Acts, the Jews (and the kingdom evangel) are set aside for a season and the uncircumcision evangel is declared by Paul to Jew and Gentile alike without distinction or preference.

In the "Circumcision Epistles" the writer of Hebrews, Peter, James, John and Jude all address the believers among Israel. Unger's Bible Handbook refers to these letters as "epistles addressed principally to Jewish believers."

BUT HAVE THE JEWS LOST THEIR CHANCE? Has "The Church" taken their place? Paul tells us that Israel has been calloused UNTIL *the complement of the nations may be entering,* after which time *all Israel shall be saved.* (Romans 11:25)

The gospels tell us of a time when the kingdom to come upon the earth was proclaimed to the Jews. Acts continues that message, even after the death and resurrection of Christ. As Acts ends Paul tells us that a new evangel is going out to Jew and Gentile alike. But when this present age has ended the kingdom evangel will once again be proclaimed upon the earth, and we see this happen in Revelation.

Has God Revealed Himself to Man?

An Overview of the Scriptures, by
BOB EVELY © *2018.*
An Independent Minister of Christ Jesus
Of the church at Wilmore, Kentucky

Before one embarks on a study of the Bible he should first consider this question: Is the Bible really God's supernatural revelation to mankind? If not, it makes no sense to spend time in serious study, as the Bible would be nothing more than a piece of historic literature much like so many others. But if the Bible truly *is* God's revelation, investing time in study is most appropriate and even necessary if we are to understand God, His purpose in creating mankind, and what lies ahead for us.

Let us begin by considering the earth and universe.

If God exists we can know of His existence even if He chose not to directly reveal Himself to us.

The house that I live in was built long ago. I have never met the builder, and suspect he is dead by now. I have no written communication from him. I have only this house that he once built.

Yet I know that the builder existed because of the visible evidence of what he once did. I know he was skilled in certain ways to be able to build a home like this ... with complicated roof-lines, a brick coal fireplace, and some mouldings and trim that are a step above the bare basics. The existence of this house is a fact. And its existence reveals to me information about the builder.

So also the world and the observable universe are facts, and evidence of its Creator. Not only can we see that a Creator has existed, but by studying and contemplating the visible creation we can draw a few conclusions about the Creator. The Creator is wise, having built into the universe much intricate detail. Everything seems to fit and work together in harmony. The Creator is mighty, having the ability to bring this massive vision into existence. Where would we begin if we chose to undertake so great a task? And the Creator was creative, as is evidenced by the beauty of the mountains, the rivers, the trees, and the many varieties of plants and flowers and birds.

So without having any further communication with man, God's fingerprint is all around us, and it reveals to us information about God, the Creator.

Now the question becomes this. Beyond this observable creation has God chosen to communicate with us? This would be His choice. If God chose not to communicate with man, we could not force Him to do so. We could merely examine the observable evidence and come to certain conclusions about God.

Many today believe this to be the case, and they believe that we can only know of God thru a study of the universe.

But the question is ... has God chosen to communicate with man on a more detailed level? Has He chosen to tell us things about Himself, or about the reason for our existence, or His plan for the universe, or what lies ahead?

To answer this question we must consider the evidence. God does not stand before us visibly, and He does not speak to us with an audible voice. But is there other evidence to consider, beyond the creation itself that might be a means thru which God has communicated with man?

Again, we cannot assume God has chosen to communicate with us at all. He may have chosen not to do so. And so we pull together the evidence that is available to us and we consider it.

What about dreams, visions and God's audible voice?

God could choose to speak to man thru dreams and visions, or thru an audible voice. Some claim that He has done so in the past, and others claim that He continues to do so in the present. And so a part of the evidence to consider is the testimony of those who claim to have heard from God thru dreams, or visions, or by hearing His voice.

But are those that tell us such things being honest, or are they fabricating stories? Or do some honestly believe they have heard from God, not knowing it was their imagination, or a mental illness, or perhaps some supernatural entity other than God?

One problem is that there are many different accounts that often conflict as to the information we are given concerning God. So how can we know which of these accounts is legitimate, if any, and which are not?

If God has chosen to reveal certain things to man, would He do so in a way that could be so confusing and so easily misunderstood, to the point that we can never really be sure what He is saying to us?

Consider your conscience!

If God created us, could it be that our conscience is the means thru which He speaks to us? This could be the means God uses to teach us what is right and what is wrong ... what is moral and what is immoral ... what is ethical and what is unethical.

But here again we have the problem of subjectivity. Each person, speaking from his own conscience, differs greatly from other persons. We can find no consensus as to absolute right and wrong.

And once again we ask ... if God has chosen to reveal things to us, would He use such a means that would be so confusing and unclear?

What about prophets?

Some say God has spoken to the mass of humanity thru certain select men and women ... prophets ... those chosen to take a message directly from God and communicate it to all others. Some say prophets existed in the past, and others say God still uses prophets today. But here, too, there is much disagreement, and many conflicting accounts from those claiming to be prophets. And if prophets are, or were, used by God ... we must have a means to discern the true prophets from the false. We must carefully consider the testimonies of those claiming to be prophets.

Now let's consider the Bible

In my lifetime I have lived in Michigan, Florida, and now Kentucky. Most of my friends and family members are Christians. I have always been taught that the Bible is God's Word revealed to mankind. I never had reason to question this, and everyone around me was so definite about the fact that the Bible is clearly God's Word. Every pastor and Bible teacher I ever encountered told me the Bible is the Word of God. Preachers pounded their pulpits and raised high their Bibles while shouting in a loud voice, "This is the Word of the Lord."

And so I can take this torch that has been passed to me and shout in an equally loud voice, "This is the Word of the Lord." I can do so because those that preceded me were so sure about the fact, as were those that preceded them, and so on. We know this is the Word of God because *everyone* knows that this is so.

But what is the _evidence_ in support of this conclusion?

Let's assume that God has chosen to reveal Himself to us thru the written word. This seems like a very good way to preserve the consistency of the message. Once recorded and preserved, it cannot shift or change as could our conscience, or the testimony of prophets, or dreams or visions.

But there is a problem! There are other writings besides the Bible that certain men claim are from God. What about the Koran? What about the Hindu scriptures? What about the Book of Mormon? What about the many others also claiming such authority?

Does it have to do with our culture? Most of those around me teach that the Bible is the Word of God. But what about those raised in Iran who are taught that the Koran is the Word of God? What about those born into the Jewish culture where everyone around them is teaching the Torah, but not the writings of the apostles? Has God blessed us with His revelation; the Bible ... while others born into other situations or cultures are being misled?

Furthermore, let us consider the Bible. Our Bible consists of 66 books that have been determined to be the Word of God. But other books were evaluated in the first few centuries of the church, and they were deemed to be uninspired and not the Word of God. But were the individuals who made these decisions correct? Did they include the correct writings? Did they leave out any? Consider that the Roman Catholic Church accepts some additional books that other Christians do not. Who is right? And consider some well-known figures from the past, like Martin Luther, who would have us remove the book of James from our Bibles if he had his way.

And so we are faced with many different writings that we must consider, and we ask the question ... is this a part of God's revelation to mankind?

But unfortunately most people today are not willing to think about the evidence. And some people want to prevent others from looking at the evidence. We are commanded to accept the fact that the Bible; or the Koran; or some other writings are from God, based on the strength of the teachers and scholars. We do not think for ourselves. And if the set of teachers and scholars around us are wrong there is no hope of finding the truth!

Consider the pressure on individuals within the various cultures of our day. If you are a Jew but become a Christian, your family and friends will disown you. If you are a Muslim and become a Christian, you might be executed. If you are a Christian but do not subscribe to what is considered to be "orthodox" beliefs, you might be asked to leave the church.

And so if God has chosen to reveal Himself to us thru the preserved written word, we have many different writings to consider as possible candidates ... and we must consider the possibility that none of them are really God's Word.

"The Bible says it ... that settles it."

Now let us consider the situation among Christian believers today. I have often heard the battle cry, "The Bible says is ... I believe it ... That settles it." This is the proof that is offered to any who might disagree.

A hundred years ago preachers could proclaim truth from the Bible, and not many would disagree; since most in our culture accepted that the Bible was the Word of God. But our culture today is different. The tide has turned, and no longer does the Bible command the respect it once had. Believers express their opinions on various issues, even quoting from the Bible, but this does not have the impact it once did.

People today are more independent, and less apt to accept a belief simply because others have passed the belief to them. It is not that they are saying, "I will not believe you, no matter what." Instead they are saying, "I will not believe you unless you can prove your point from the evidence." But Christians today are not ready for this challenge. The average Believer today does not know *why* he believes the things he believes. And if the average person were to really think about why they believe, they would be forced to admit they are basing their beliefs on things that have been taught to them by others.

There is the story of a newly married bride preparing a pot roast for her husband, and she begins by cutting both ends off the roast. When her watchful husband asks why she has done this, she replies that this is just how you prepare a roast, and when pressed further she does not really know why. When the young woman calls her mother to ask why it is that both ends must be cut off from the roast her mother replies, "Because the pan that I always used was small, and I had to cut off the ends to make the roast fit."

We often believe what we believe without really knowing *why* we believe it.

Could we be false witnesses?
If we make claims about God to the world based on the Bible, we had better know for certain that the Bible is God's Word and that we are properly understanding it; or we could be false witnesses. We could actually be *opposing* God, all the while thinking we are speaking *for* Him.

Those of us who believe the Bible is God's Word are familiar with Saul, who later became Paul. Before Paul's Damascus Road experience, he was passionately doing what he believed was God's work. No one could have convinced him that he was on the wrong side, as he physically pulled Christians from their homes to persecute them or to kill them for proclaiming the name of Jesus Christ. Paul was devoted, and zealous, and sincere, and passionate about his beliefs ... and he thought we was speaking for God. But he was wrong.

I wonder how many there are in the world today just like Paul prior to his experience on the road to Damascus. False witnesses; proclaiming things about God that are not true!

Let us consider the evidence.
To thoroughly consider the issue of God's revealed Word to man; which writings are a part of His Word and which are not; we would need to lay out all of the possible manuscripts before us and study them, looking for evidence. This would be an arduous task, since many of the candidates would

be hard to find and possibly corrupted since the time they were first written, and since we would need to have knowledge of a number of different languages to properly study them.

But if we do not undertake this task, how can we really weigh all of the evidence to know what is, and what is not, God's Word?

Consider the perfection in the basic message being conveyed.

Without studying in detail each of the various writings that have been raised as a possible candidate, we consider the basic message being conveyed by each. And when we do so we will find in the Bible a wisdom higher than any human wisdom; and much different than any other writing claiming scriptural authority. Consider the explanation found in the Bible concerning that state of man, and man's destiny.

God creates all things, including mankind. Man has a close fellowship with God, until man sins and death is the result. Humanity inherits this death condition; this mortality. God speaks not to the mass of humanity with an audible voice, but to select individuals that He chooses to be His instruments. Signs and wonders validate their message to enable mankind to differentiate between the true prophets and those that are false. God communicates His just requirements to mankind, but time and again mankind fails to be righteous. Experience proves that none have the ability to be righteous according to God's standards. All appears to be lost.

God does not choose a select group *exclusively*, as some erroneously teach; or as some other belief systems teach. God's purpose is always to bless ALL of mankind. But His means for doing so is to work thru certain select individuals who are called to be His instruments. Abraham, Isaac and Jacob were God's instruments, and God communicated directly with them. But always, the Bible tells us, God's intent is to bless all mankind.

Jacob is renamed Israel, and his descendants become known as the Israelites. Thru Moses the Law is given to the Israelites. Always God desires to bless all mankind, but His chosen instrument; the nation of Israel; fails to be faithful. Israel is removed from her land, and the line of kings ends as the nation is in exile. But even then God speaks thru His prophets of a time when Israel would be restored to her land, and when the Anointed One would come and reign upon the throne.

John the Baptist comes bearing the message that the kingdom is near and it is time to repent and get ready. Jesus follows with the same message; the kingdom is near. Here was the Anointed One, ready to fulfill the words of the prophets by sitting upon the throne to reign, and thru Israel all peoples upon the earth would be blessed.

But Israel does not recognize the time of the king's visitation. The kingdom is rejected, and the king is crucified.

The apostles continue proclaiming the coming kingdom message TO THE NATION OF ISRAEL. Peter calls upon Israel to repent so that the times of restoration that were spoken of by the prophets could come, and so that the Anointed One would return.

But again and again Israel rejects the message, and persecutes those who proclaim it.

Since the day God told Abraham, "All peoples of the earth will be blessed through you," God has been working thru His chosen instruments to accomplish this very purpose. But His instruments have not cooperated. It appears that God's plan is at an impasse. How can the kingdom come upon the earth, and how can God bless all peoples thru Israel, when Israel herself continues to reject the message from God?

But this too is a part of God's plan. This rejection may not have been prophesied before, but it fits right into God's plan for the ages. Israel rejects the kingdom, so God now turns directly to the Gentiles. Paul is not one of the select twelve apostles; but he is an apostle chosen by God nonetheless. He is an apostle of a different kind, and he did not simply continue the same message that had been borne by the others who preceded him. When Paul became a believer he did not study under the other believers. This might have seemed like a good idea in the ways of man, but God had different plans; and He revealed new things directly to Paul; things that had not been revealed to mankind ever before.

God is no longer working thru Israel as His instrument. He now goes directly to Gentiles, who are joint heirs (equals) with Israel. The focus is no longer on Israel being born again, but on an entirely *new creation*. No longer is the focus on the nearness of the kingdom to come upon the earth; but upon God's broader kingdom overarching the entire universe. No longer do we wait for the Lord to come to reign upon the earth; we wait for Him to call us to meet Him in the air.

But God has not rejected Israel forever. Israel will still serve a purpose when Christ prepares to return to establish the kingdom upon the earth. But for now Israel has been temporarily set aside as God works thru a new instrument; an instrument that had not been mentioned by the prophets of old; the Body of Christ. This new instrument is the example of God's grace to the entire world.

The day will come when Christ descends, when the trumpet sounds, and when the Body of Christ is called to be with Him to play a part in the heavens. And the day will come when Christ returns to reign upon the earth, when again Israel will play a part. And the day will come when all of God's creation will be subjected to Him, under the reign of Christ, when all are reconciled to God; when not one sheep remains lost; when even death and evil are defeated; when all are saved; and when God becomes All in all.

It all began with God alone, in perfection. Man is on a journey, guided by the sovereign God, toward a perfect conclusion.

When we step back and consider this revelation, can any dispute the wisdom and love and power that prevails? Just as God's fingerprint is upon His visible creation, letting us know that He *does* exist and did create all that we see around us ... so also God's fingerprint is upon the Word of God when we consider the wisdom, the genius and the perfection of the message.

When we consider the other writings that some claim are from God, we know enough of the message being conveyed to see that there is not the same wisdom and perfection that permeates the Bible. In no other case do we see the perfection of God, the flaws of mankind, and the perfect plan where not just some; but _all_ of creation is reconciled to God, ending in perfection.

And so the wisdom and perfection of what is revealed in the Bible is evidence that this is God's revelation to man.

Consider the Bible's unity
As we consider the Bible's account, ending with total reconciliation and perfection, we note the unity found throughout. Despite the fact that many different human agents were at work in relaying God's message to us, and despite the fact that the various accounts were penned at different times there is a wonderful unity that exists when we consider the account as a whole. Each chapter and verse exists with purpose, and helps to form the total unified whole.

Furthermore, there is a _progressive revelation_ throughout time as God's plans unfold. The judges reveal more of God's truth than the patriarchs possessed; and the prophets reveal more than the judges.

Consider prophecy.
Look at the many prophecies found in Scripture that have been fulfilled to the last detail! In "God's Eonian Purpose," Mr. Adlai Loudy observes:

> "... twenty five specific predictions were made by the Hebrew prophets, bearing on the betrayal, trial, death, and burial of Christ. These were uttered by different

prophets during a period of five hundred years ... yet they were all fulfilled in twenty four hours in one person – the Christ of Whom they spoke." (p 27)

Would man have recorded his history in this way?

As we consider the story of mankind as found in the Bible we must ask the question; would man have told the story in this way if left to himself? Even the greatest of men is shown to be fallible and sinful. Even those who preceded Christ in His geneology are filled with flaws.

The blatantly honest manner in which mankind is described is evidence that the hand of God was at work in this revelation.

But do we have the correct 66 books?

We still have the problem that fallible men made the selection as to what to include and what not to include in the Bible, and we are placing faith in them as to these decisions.

I recommend a most excellent book, "The Original Bible Restored" by Ernest Martin. Martin provides evidence that the Bible was "canonized" (approval of which books to include) by the apostles themselves, long before the church councils. The Old Testament canonization process began with Hezekiah when Judah was in danger of being destroyed, and then finalized by Ezra. Both used a "signature" consisting of certain Hebrew letters or phrases to confirm the legitimate writings to include.

Because Ezra was facing a proliferation of false religious beliefs and customs caused by intermarriage, he selected the books to be included in the Old Testament canon, and he arranged them in proper order. Interestingly, he canonized 22 books ... the same exact writings we have in our Old Testaments today; but with some books that were divided at a later time (e.g. Joshua and Judges which were a single book in Ezra's canon). The significance of 22 books? In Hebrew acrostics (a form of poetry) there were always 22 sentences, one for each letter in the Hebrew alphabet. And so 22 would be a sign of completion.

Turning now to the New Testament, the later writings of the apostles talk of a growing turning away from the truth, and this seems to have been their motivation for sealing the legitimate writings for believers after their deaths. John reported that rebels had infiltrated the church (1 John 2:18,19) and that many were no longer listening to or submitting to the original apostles. (1 John 4:6) Some elders within the church were rejecting John's authority. (3 John 9,10) Peter writes that destructive sects would soon rise from within the church, even denying Christ's return. (2 Peter 2:1,2,13; 3:3,4) He describes an apostasy from the truth and warns against the coming errors. (2 Peter 3:17)

Peter said there would be false teachers (2 Peter 2:1) and that many would follow them. When Jude later wrote his letter, these things had already begun.

It is also clear that Paul's main desire was that sound doctrine be preserved following his death, as there would be a great falling away from the truth. (2 Timothy 4:1-8) When Paul summoned Timothy and Mark to Rome with the scrolls and vellums (probably certain specific writings), this was probably a part of the canonization process. With Mark being a close associate of Peter's, Martin contends that Paul probably used this occasion to send his inspired writings to Peter for inclusion in the canon.

Luke reported that many were composing "gospels" (Luke 1:1) and since these were being written in a time of growing rebellion, how could one be certain these gospels were accurate accounts?

So recognizing that Christ's return was not imminent as they once thought, and seeing the growth of false doctrines and a general turning away from the truth, the apostles began to see the need to preserve the truth for the future church. There needed to be an official written document finalized before their deaths.

Think about this. Seeing the need to preserve truth, and observing the falling away from truth as their lives and ministries moved toward the end, would it make sense that the apostles would simply die and let others formulate the official canon? If they couldn't trust the doctrines of many in their midst even as they lived, how could they depend on the church at a future time to preserve the written truth?

One final note from Martin's book. When we consider the 22 books in the original Old Testament canon and the 27 books in the New Testament canon, we have 49 books in total ... 7 times 7 which represents completion and perfection. This would seem to be a validation of the legitimacy of the canon. It is a shame that this validation is more difficult to see after the tampering of the later church brought the number to 66 books.

I have included here just a brief snapshot of some of Martin's key points in "The Original Bible Restored," and I would highly recommend that the reader seek out a copy of this excellent book to read in full.

Let me also recommend the writings of EW Bullinger and AE Knoch.
Both of these men have done a very intricate analysis of the Bible. In the extensive writings of both Bullinger and Knoch, who worked independently of one another, we are provided with very detailed outlines of the Bible that show great symmetry and perfection. While the overall message being

conveyed by the Bible shows great wisdom and perfection, so also does a literary analysis of the writings themselves.

And as observed previously, the Bible presents us with an honest, unified, complete picture of mankind; from creation to a perfect reconciliation, despite the sinfulness and helplessness of man.

Were there additional writings that were left out and not included? If there were, I don't believe it would be possible for us today to find them. And again pointing to the perfection of what we have with us today in the 66 books we call the Bible, it would seem that the complete account has been preserved for us.

What about the many different translations and interpretations of the Bible?

Everything I have stated thus far is dependent on our having an accurate translation from the original languages, and an accurate interpretation of what the Bible is teaching.

Unfortunately the issue becomes clouded by the many different Bible translations today which are focused more on being easy to read than being faithful to the original manuscripts. These translations differ from one another, and they make certain passages appear to contradict other passages.

Coupled with this is the problem of interpretation. Today we have many different denominations, and many different preachers, scholars, teachers and writers ... and while they all start with the same Bible, they teach many drastically different things, contradicting one another. This confusion makes it appear that the Bible is not the Word of God, because supposedly learned men cannot agree what it says.

The perfection of the message is lost when we rely upon the imperfect teachings of men as to what the Bible says. Far from the perfection that is revealed in God's Word, we hear instead of a God Who loves the world (all mankind) but Who is willing to torment some forever and ever. We hear of a God Who says on the one hand that He will seek the single lost sheep until it is found, while also saying that some of the lost will remain lost forever and ever. We hear of a God who will deal with a man who commits a finite amount of sin in this short lifetime by tormenting him with an infinite punishment, forever and ever.

Many believers today proclaim an imperfect and illogical message, and as a result many do not believe the Bible can possibly be God's Word. But it is not God's Word that is the problem; it is the traditions and teachings of men that have crept into the English translation of the Bible, and the many divergent and contradictory teachings being proclaimed today.

Many today teach, supposedly from God's Word,

> That God created all things,
>
> That God is in control of all things,
>
> That God is love,
>
> That God created man and placed him upon this earth which is filled with temptation and evil,
>
> That God sent His Son to die for the sins of man ...
>
> BUT
>
> In the end some will accept Him and some will reject Him,
>
> And the story will end with a lake of fire tormenting some forever and ever,
>
> While those that believed in their lifetime spend eternity in heaven enjoying their reward

A perfect God; with an imperfect plan that cannot or will not reconcile ALL, but only some. Even if we try to pin the blame on man for failing to believe; the fact is that God could not develop a plan that would ultimately reconcile all of His creation to Himself, even though that is His desire. (1 Timothy 2:4)

It is easy to see why this prevailing message of Christianity today is leading people to the conclusion that the Bible is NOT the Word of God. But when carefully and consistently translated, and when carefully and thoughtfully studied and contemplated; apart from the biased teachings of man; we cannot fail to appreciate the wisdom of God as revealed in His revelation to man.

Can the majority of believers be wrong?

Some will counter by asking how such a minority viewpoint can be correct, when nearly the entire church in all of its denominations teaches of an eternal hell.

My response would be to point to the Bible itself, and to ask when the truth was ever in the majority. When the Old Testament prophets spoke, were they in the majority? When John the Baptist spoke, was he in the majority? When Jesus went up against the Pharisees, was He in the majority? And even at the end of Paul's ministry, when he arrived in Jerusalem and was arrested to be taken to Rome, he was in the minority. Paul was opposed not just by the unbelieving Jews, but also by those who believed but who were zealous for the law and who objected to his teachings concerning grace. (Acts 21:20)

In all of Scripture, when was the majority correct? Today we hear believers marvel that this huge church has grown from such a small number of persecuted believers in that early church we read about in the Bible. But as the church has grown, and as "orthodoxy" was defined by the church fathers in the 5th century; what makes us think that the majority opinion is correct?

Is it possible to study God's Word objectively today?

Some that I have encountered will fatalistically declare that even if the ultimate salvation of all is true, it is impossible for the average person today to come to this conclusion.

But if one is willing to accept the fact that the majority opinion of the church, commonly referred to as "orthodoxy," could perhaps be incorrect, and if he is willing to study the Word of God for himself; then God's plan to ultimately save all of mankind is clear and obvious. What prevents this from happening is the fact that most have been "indoctrinated" into a system of beliefs that is prevalent in their church, denomination, or circle of friends; and the Bible is studied in light of that context, instead of objectively. In other words, opinions are already determined before Bible study begins, and the Bible is simply used to prove that the pre-determined opinions are correct. Most begin from the perspective that there is an eternal hell, a place of endless torment, and this viewpoint is then proven from the Bible, while setting aside or limiting passages that seem to contradict the viewpoint.

I wish to express my sincere appreciation for the work of Mr. A E. Knoch and the others that were associated with him. I am not a follower of Mr. Knoch as others might follow Luther or Calvin or Wesley. If I led others to follow Mr. Knoch, I would be no different than those who are dependent upon the teachings of a certain man.

But I will point to the method used by Mr. Knoch, and say that this method is the best approach for translating Scripture, casting off the biases of mankind as much as is humanly possible, to study from the pure Word of God; without knowing the original languages.

If God wanted to reveal Himself, how would He have done so?

Think about something. If God did choose to reveal things to man, would he do so by ensuring that His Word was recorded in a consistent and clear manner, or would He allow the individual men who recorded His message to do so in an inconsistent manner?

Again quoting from "God's Eonian Purpose" by Mr. Loudy:

"... thought can only be expressed in words, and those words must express the exact thought of the speaker, otherwise, his exact thought is not expressed." (p 24)

"'Have a pattern of sound words which you hear from me' (2 Timothy 1:13). Thus we see that inerrancy demands that the sacred scribe be simply an amanuensis, and given the exact words. And this is confirmed by the Scriptures themselves, as in 2 Peter 1:21, 'For prophecy was not at any time carried on by the will of man, but holy men of God speak, being carried on by holy spirit.'"

If God was not clear and consistent in His message, how would we know today what He was trying to tell us? The fact is that if we will carefully study God's Word, we will marvel at its consistency.

I do not use the Concordant Version of the Bible simply because I think it is a better translation than any other. This would be basing my choice on personal preference, much like someone would choose the Living Bible versus the NIV versus the New King James, and so on.

I use the Concordant Version because of the METHOD that was used.

Look at almost any other translation and you see great inconsistency. A single word, like aion, is sometimes translated eternal, sometimes age, sometimes world. Would God have His chosen writers pass His Word to us so inconsistently? The problem is the bias of man that has crept in. If the translator, based on his understanding of the Bible as taught to him, thinks the word "world" fits better in one particular context because the word "eternal" won't fit; he makes this decision. And all who study from his Bible translation are now affected by this decision.

Or consider the example of hell. Here we have a Hebrew word (sheol) and three totally different Greek words (hades, gehenna, tartarus) and all are simply mixed together indiscriminately into a single English word "hell." But even more inconsistent are those cases when one of these words, like "hades" or "sheol", is found and which cannot possibly mean "hell" as we understand "hell" to be ... so the translator must resort to another word in this case; something like "grave."

A wise God seeks to reveal Himself to mankind by using sound words so we can understand what He is telling us ... but His word is handled carelessly and inconsistently, and distorted to fit the teachings of mankind.

I use the Concordant Version because it is *consistent*, and it enables me to look at any English word that was used; tracing it to the original Greek word; examining how that same Greek word was used in all other instances; and knowing when the original writers were using the same words or different words to express their thoughts.

It is only when we use a translation in our study that has taken such steps to be consistent, that we can fully observe and appreciate the perfection of God's revelation to mankind.

Think for yourself!

These, then are the evidences I have considered. I have told you why I have come to the conclusion that the Bible is the Word of God; and the message I see God relaying to mankind in His Word. Now I ask you to consider all evidence available and to come to your own conclusions. Do not believe these things I have said simply because I believe them, or even because I might sound convincing. And do not think I am wrong simply because of the opinions you have been taught by others through the years that you think to be "experts."

As we consider the question, "Has God revealed Himself to us?" I ask that you consider the evidence, study, discuss, contemplate, pray, and *think for yourself.*

Index

This overview contains the thoughts and opinions of the author, and is a work in progress as his study of the Scriptures continues. Some things that God has revealed are very clear. That Christ died for our sins; that He was entombed; and that He was roused (1 Corinthians 15:3) is clear. That all are to be ultimately reconciled to God thru the work of Christ is also very clear (1 Corinthians 15:20-28). But on many specifics in the Scriptures there are a variety of interpretations and opinions, and none should conclude they have the complete and final understanding on these matters that are less clear. The reader is encouraged to consider various opinions, but to study and to think for himself. Within the Body of Christ we should study and discuss our understandings so as to mutually reach a more complete understanding of that which God has revealed.

Unless otherwise noted, Scriptures are taken from the Concordant Literal New Testament and the Concordant Version of the Old Testament. Concordant Publishing Concern, 15570 West Knochaven Road, Santa Clarita, CA 91387 (www.Concordant.org)

Grace Evangel Fellowship:
P O Box 6, Wilmore, KY 40390
www.GraceEvangel.org

About the Author

Bob Evely is Vice President with a national company, overseeing sales, sales training, servicing, marketing, and special projects. He is a graduate of Oakland University (Rochester, Michigan) and has a Master of Divinity (M.Div.) Degree from Asbury Theological Seminary (Wilmore, Kentucky). For three and a half years Bob served as pastor of the Canton and West Point United Methodist Churches in Salem, Indiana; and for five years he served as pastor of the Open Door Free Methodist Church in Nicholasville, Kentucky. Both were bi-vocational positions, with Bob supporting his family through full time employment.

In May 2002 Bob resigned as pastor of Open Door Free Methodist Church to found Grace Evangel Fellowship, an independent ministry/church based in Wilmore, Kentucky. His ministry includes writing, speaking, teaching, and corresponding via email.

Bob resides in Wilmore, Kentucky with his wife Jill (since 1975). Originally from the Romeo, Michigan area the Evelys have five children: Cris (Jen), Dusty (Sharon), Chad (Molly), Kari (Jason), and Scott (Martha). As of this writing they are blessed with 7 grandchildren (Elinor, Allison, Abby, Lilli, Livi, Annabelle, and Alex).

Jill homeschooled all five children, and for 20 years represented Sonlight Curriculum as a consultant. Besides staying busy as a wife, mother, and grandma, Jill is an accomplished soap maker (PrairieKari.com) and she continues to encourage parents interested in homeschooling their children.

The author can be contacted at Grace Evangel Fellowship, P O Box 6, Wilmore, Kentucky 40390; or via email bob@GraceEvangel.org

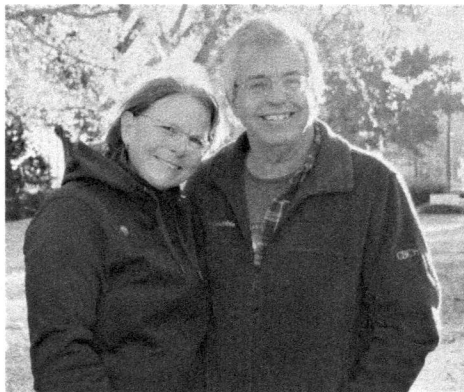

Books by Bob Evely

At the End of the Ages; the Abolition of Hell (2002)

The Visitation; An Overview of the New Testament, Part One (2018)

The Waiting; An Overview of the New Testament, Part Two (2018)

The Pause; An Overview of the New Testament, Part Three (2018)

The Return of the King; An Overview of the New Testament, Part Four (2018)

Many shorter writings can be found at GraceEvangel.org

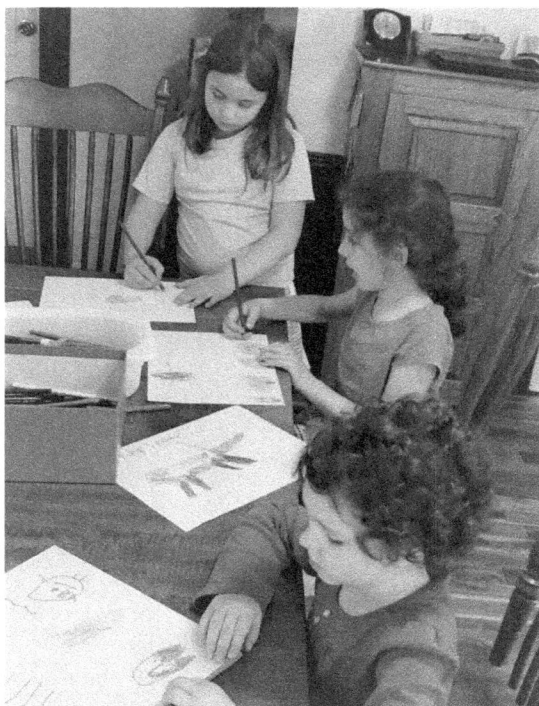

Book Artists at Work
Allison, Elinor & Lilli Evely